LINUX

From Installation to Advanced System Administration

Rama Nolan

Table of Contents

Introduction

Linux, an open-source operating system, has its roots in the early 1990s. The story of Linux begins with a young computer science student named Linus Torvalds, who started developing the kernel, the core of the operating system, as a personal project in 1991. Torvalds was inspired by the MINIX operating system, a Unix-like system created by Professor Andrew Tanenbaum for educational purposes. However, MINIX had its limitations, and Torvalds aimed to create a free and open-source alternative that would be more robust and versatile.

Torvalds initially released the Linux kernel under a proprietary license but quickly realized that for the operating system to grow and evolve, it needed to be open to contributions from other developers. In September 1991, he re-released Linux under the GNU General Public License (GPL), a pivotal moment that allowed anyone to modify, distribute, and use the software freely. This decision marked the beginning of the Linux operating system as a collaborative effort, with developers worldwide contributing to its development.

As Linux grew in popularity, it began to incorporate components from the GNU Project, a free software initiative started by Richard Stallman in 1983. The combination of the Linux kernel and GNU tools resulted in what is commonly referred to as a "Linux distribution," an operating system that includes the Linux kernel and a collection of software that makes the system functional and user-friendly.

Linux's evolution has been shaped by the contributions of a global community of developers, as well as the support of major technology companies. Over the years, Linux has grown from a hobbyist project into a powerful and versatile operating system used in a wide range of environments, from personal computers to enterprise servers, and from smartphones to supercomputers.

The development of Linux distributions, such as Debian, Red Hat, Ubuntu, and Fedora, has further contributed to its widespread adoption. These distributions package the Linux kernel with various software applications, making Linux accessible to users with different needs and expertise levels. Each distribution has its unique features, target audience, and use cases, catering to a diverse range of users, from beginners to advanced system administrators.

Linux's open-source nature has made it a favorite in the tech community, fostering innovation and enabling rapid development. The operating system's modularity, stability, and security have made it a popular choice for servers, data centers, and cloud computing environments. Additionally, Linux's flexibility has led to its adoption in embedded systems, such as routers, smart devices, and automotive systems.

In recent years, Linux has also gained traction in the desktop market, thanks to user-friendly distributions like Ubuntu and Linux Mint. These distributions have made Linux more accessible to everyday users, offering a viable alternative to proprietary operating systems like Windows and macOS.

The rise of Linux in the enterprise space has been significant, with many organizations opting for Linux servers due to their cost-effectiveness, reliability, and scalability. The operating system's role in the development of open-source software, cloud computing, and containerization technologies, such as Docker and Kubernetes, has further solidified its position as a critical player in the tech industry.

As Linux continues to evolve, its impact on the world of computing remains profound. The operating system's principles of openness, collaboration, and innovation continue to drive its development, ensuring that Linux will remain a cornerstone of modern technology for years to come.

Overview of Linux Distributions

Linux distributions, or "distros," are versions of the Linux operating system that package the Linux kernel with a variety of software applications, tools, and utilities. Each distribution is tailored to meet specific needs, ranging from general-purpose desktop use to specialized server environments. The diversity of Linux distributions allows users to choose a version that best suits their requirements, whether they are developers, system administrators, or everyday users.

Popular Linux Distributions

1. Ubuntu

One of the most popular and user-friendly Linux distributions, Ubuntu is based on Debian. It's known for its ease of use, regular updates, and strong community support. Ubuntu is a great choice for beginners and is widely used on desktops, servers, and cloud environments.

2. Debian

Debian is known for its stability and robust package management system. It is a non-commercial distribution that serves as the foundation for many other distributions, including Ubuntu. Debian is preferred by users who value a rock-solid and secure operating system.

3. Fedora

Sponsored by Red Hat, Fedora focuses on cutting-edge technologies and serves as a testing ground for features that may eventually be included in Red Hat Enterprise Linux (RHEL).

Fedora is often used by developers and tech enthusiasts who want to experiment with the latest innovations.

4. Red Hat Enterprise Linux (RHEL)

RHEL is a commercial distribution designed for enterprise environments. It offers long-term support, stability, and a wide range of enterprise-grade tools and services. RHEL is widely used in corporate data centers and mission-critical applications.

5. CentOS

CentOS was a free and community-supported version of RHEL, offering the same features and stability without the commercial support. However, CentOS has transitioned to CentOS Stream, a rolling-release distribution that serves as the upstream for RHEL.

6. Linux Mint

Based on Ubuntu, Linux Mint provides a familiar user interface for those transitioning from Windows. It's known for its simplicity, elegance, and full multimedia support out-of-the-box, making it a popular choice for desktop users.

7. Arch Linux

Arch Linux is a lightweight and flexible distribution that follows a rolling release model. It is designed for users who prefer to build their system from the ground up, offering a minimalistic base and the ability to customize every aspect of the system.

8. SUSE Linux Enterprise Server (SLES)

SLES is a commercial distribution designed for enterprise environments, similar to RHEL. It's known for its scalability, security, and support for mission-critical workloads. SUSE is particularly strong in the European market.

9. Kali Linux

Kali Linux is a specialized distribution designed for security professionals and ethical hackers. It comes pre-installed with a wide range of security tools for penetration testing, forensic analysis, and network security.

Specialized Distributions

In addition to general-purpose distributions, there are specialized distros tailored for specific tasks or environments. For example, **Raspberry Pi OS** is optimized for the Raspberry Pi hardware, while **Tails** is designed for secure and anonymous internet browsing. These specialized distributions allow Linux to be used in a wide variety of scenarios, from embedded systems to digital forensics.

Why Choose Linux: Advantages in Various Environments

Linux offers a wide range of advantages that make it an appealing choice for different environments, from personal desktops to enterprise servers and cloud computing.

1. Security

Linux is renowned for its security features. The open-source nature of Linux allows for continuous inspection and auditing by developers worldwide, which helps to identify and patch vulnerabilities more quickly than in closed-source systems. Additionally, Linux's permission and user privilege systems make it inherently more secure against malware and unauthorized access.

2. Stability and Reliability

Linux is known for its stability and reliability, particularly in server environments. It is common for Linux servers to run for years without requiring a reboot, making it ideal for mission-critical applications where uptime is essential. The robust file system and process management in Linux contribute to its stability, preventing system crashes and data corruption.

3. Cost-Effectiveness

Most Linux distributions are free to download and use, making it a cost-effective solution for individuals, businesses, and educational institutions. This significantly reduces the total cost of ownership (TCO) for systems running Linux, especially when compared to proprietary operating systems that require licensing fees.

4. Customizability

One of the most significant advantages of Linux is its flexibility and customizability. Users have complete control over the operating system, allowing them to modify and optimize it for specific tasks. Whether it's changing the desktop environment, tweaking system settings, or building a custom kernel, Linux provides the tools and freedom to create a personalized experience.

5. Strong Community Support

Linux has a vast and active community of users and developers who contribute to its continuous improvement. This community-driven approach ensures that support is readily available through forums, online documentation, and user groups. The collaborative nature of Linux development also means that updates and new features are frequently released.

6. Open-Source Ecosystem

As an open-source operating system, Linux is part of a broader ecosystem of open-source software. This ecosystem includes thousands of applications, tools, and utilities that are also free to use and modify. The open-source model fosters innovation and ensures that users are not locked into proprietary solutions.

7. Compatibility and Performance

Linux is highly compatible with a wide range of hardware, from the latest high-performance servers to older, resource-constrained devices. This compatibility, combined with the lightweight nature of many Linux distributions, ensures that Linux can run efficiently on virtually any system. Additionally, Linux is often preferred for high-performance computing tasks due to its ability to handle large workloads and optimize system resources.

8. Versatility in Different Environments

Linux's versatility is evident in its widespread use across different environments. On the desktop, distributions like Ubuntu and Linux Mint offer a user-friendly experience for everyday computing. In enterprise environments, distributions like RHEL and SLES provide the stability, security, and support needed for large-scale deployments. In the cloud, Linux is the dominant operating system, powering the majority of servers on platforms like AWS, Azure, and Google Cloud.

9. Ideal for Developers

Linux is the preferred platform for many developers due to its rich set of development tools, support for multiple programming languages, and compatibility with version control systems like Git. The command-line interface (CLI) in Linux is particularly powerful, enabling developers to automate tasks, manage software, and deploy applications efficiently.

10. Environmentally Friendly

Linux's efficiency and ability to run on older hardware extend the lifecycle of devices, reducing electronic waste. By breathing new life into aging systems, Linux helps promote sustainability and environmental responsibility.

In summary, Linux's combination of security, stability, cost-effectiveness, and versatility makes it an ideal operating system for a wide range of environments. Whether you're a developer, a system administrator, or a casual user, Linux provides the tools and flexibility to meet your needs.

Installing Linux

Choosing the Right Linux Distribution for Your Needs

Selecting the right Linux distribution is a crucial first step in your journey with Linux. With a plethora of distributions available, each tailored to different needs, it's essential to understand which one aligns best with your requirements. Whether you're a beginner, a developer, a system administrator, or someone looking to repurpose an old machine, there's a Linux distribution out there for you.

Identifying Your Use Case

The first step in choosing a Linux distribution is to identify your specific use case. Consider the following scenarios:

- For General Desktop Use: If you're looking for a user-friendly operating system for everyday tasks like browsing, document editing, and media consumption, distributions like Ubuntu, Linux Mint, and Fedora are excellent choices. These distributions offer a polished graphical interface, strong community support, and a wide range of pre-installed applications.
- For Development: If you're a developer, you might prefer a distribution that provides easy access to development tools, libraries, and programming environments. Fedora, Ubuntu, and Arch Linux are popular among developers due to their cutting-edge software repositories and strong support for multiple programming languages.
- For System Administration: For those managing servers or enterprise environments, stability, security, and long-term support are critical. Red Hat Enterprise Linux (RHEL),

CentOS Stream, and SUSE Linux Enterprise Server (SLES) are designed for such environments, offering robust performance and enterprise-grade support.

- For Older Hardware: If you have an older machine with limited resources, lightweight distributions like Lubuntu, Xubuntu, or Puppy Linux can breathe new life into your hardware. These distributions are optimized to run on minimal resources while still providing a full-featured desktop experience.
- For Security and Privacy: If your focus is on security and privacy, distributions like Kali Linux for penetration testing and Tails for anonymous web browsing are specialized tools built with these goals in mind.
- For Educational Purposes: If you're using Linux for educational purposes or want to introduce others to Linux, distributions like Edubuntu or Sugar on a Stick are designed with education in mind, providing tools and applications geared towards learning environments.

Considering the User Interface

Linux distributions offer various desktop environments, each with its unique look and feel. The desktop environment determines how you interact with your system, including the taskbar, application menus, and window management. Some popular desktop environments include:

- GNOME: Known for its simplicity and modern design, GNOME is the default environment for Ubuntu and Fedora. It offers a clean, streamlined interface that's easy to navigate.
- KDE Plasma: KDE provides a highly customizable and feature-rich interface, making it a favorite for users who prefer control over every aspect of their desktop.

- Xfce: Lightweight and fast, Xfce is ideal for users who want a responsive system without sacrificing too many features.
- LXQt: LXQt is another lightweight desktop environment, often paired with distributions like Lubuntu, that focuses on efficiency and speed.

Evaluating Package Management and Software Repositories

Different distributions use different package management systems and software repositories. The package manager is the tool you'll use to install, update, and manage software on your Linux system. Some common package managers include:

- APT (Advanced Package Tool): Used by Debian-based distributions like Ubuntu and Linux Mint, APT is known for its ease of use and large software repositories.
- YUM/DNF: These are used by Red Hat-based distributions like Fedora and CentOS Stream. DNF, the successor to YUM, is powerful and efficient for managing software on your system.
- Pacman: The package manager for Arch Linux, Pacman, is known for its simplicity and speed. It provides access to the Arch User Repository (AUR), which contains a vast collection of user-maintained packages.
- ZYpp: Used by SUSE-based distributions, ZYpp is known for its robustness and reliability in managing packages and dependencies.

When choosing a distribution, consider the package manager you're most comfortable with and the availability of the software you need in the distribution's repositories.

Community Support and Documentation

The strength of a distribution's community and the quality of its documentation are vital factors, especially for beginners. Distributions like Ubuntu, Fedora, and Arch Linux have large, active communities and extensive documentation, making it easier to find help and troubleshoot issues.

Long-Term Support (LTS) vs. Rolling Releases

Another important consideration is whether you prefer a distribution with Long-Term Support (LTS) or a rolling release model:

- LTS Distributions: LTS versions of distributions like Ubuntu are supported for several years with security updates and bug fixes. They're ideal for users who prioritize stability and don't want to upgrade frequently.
- Rolling Release Distributions: Rolling release distributions like Arch Linux continuously update to the latest versions of software and the operating system itself. This model is ideal for users who want access to the latest features and are comfortable with frequent updates.

Testing and Trying Out Distributions

Before committing to a distribution, it's a good idea to test it out. Many distributions offer live CDs or USBs, allowing you to run the operating system from external media without installing it. This gives you the opportunity to explore the user interface, test compatibility with your hardware, and see if it meets your needs.

Once you've selected a distribution, you're ready to move on to the installation process, which will be covered in detail in the next sections. Choosing the right Linux distribution is a personal decision, but with the wide array of options available, you're sure to find one that fits your requirements perfectly.

Step-by-Step Guide to Installing Linux on Different Platforms

Installing Linux can be a straightforward process, whether you're setting it up on a desktop, laptop, or even a virtual machine. This guide will walk you through the steps to install Linux on various platforms, ensuring you have a smooth experience regardless of your hardware setup.

Preparing for Installation

Before installing Linux, it's essential to prepare your system and gather the necessary tools:

- Back Up Your Data: If you're installing Linux on a system that already has an operating system, ensure you back up any important data. While the installation process is generally safe, it's always better to be cautious.
- Download the Linux Distribution: Visit the official website of the Linux distribution you've chosen (e.g., Ubuntu, Fedora, Arch Linux) and download the ISO file. This file is a disk image that you'll use to create a bootable installation media.
- Create a Bootable USB Drive or DVD: To install Linux, you'll need to create a bootable USB drive or DVD. Tools like Rufus (for Windows), Etcher (for Windows, macOS, and Linux), or **UNetbootin can help you create a bootable USB drive from the ISO file. If you prefer, you can burn the ISO file to a DVD.

Installing Linux on a Desktop or Laptop

The process of installing Linux on a desktop or laptop is similar across most distributions. Here's how to do it:

Step 1: Boot from the Installation Media

- Insert the USB Drive or DVD: Plug in your bootable USB drive or insert the DVD into the computer where you want to install Linux.
- Restart Your Computer: Restart the system and enter the BIOS/UEFI settings by pressing a key (often F2, F12, DEL, or ESC) during the boot process. Refer to your computer's manual for the exact key.
- Change Boot Order: In the BIOS/UEFI settings, change the boot order to prioritize booting from the USB drive or DVD.
- Save and Exit: Save the changes and exit the BIOS/UEFI settings. Your computer should now boot from the USB drive or DVD.

Step 2: Start the Installation Process

- Select the Installation Mode: After booting, you'll see a welcome screen with options like "Try Linux" or "Install Linux." If you want to test the distribution first, choose "Try Linux." Otherwise, select "Install Linux" to begin the installation.
- Choose Language and Keyboard Layout: Follow the on-screen prompts to select your preferred language and keyboard layout.
- Prepare the Disk: You'll be asked how you want to install Linux:

  - Install alongside existing OS: If you want to dual-boot Linux with another OS (like Windows), choose this option.

  - Erase disk and install Linux: This will erase the entire disk and install Linux as the only operating system.

  - Something else: For advanced users who want to manually partition the disk.

- Set Up Partitions: If you selected "Something else," you'll need to manually set up partitions:

  - Root (/): The main partition for the OS. Allocate at least 20 GB.

  - Home (/home): A separate partition for user data (optional but recommended).

  - Swap: Used as virtual memory. Allocate a swap size equal to your RAM size.

- Create a User Account: You'll be prompted to create a username and password. This will be your primary account on the system.
- Select Time Zone: Choose your time zone to configure system time.

Step 3: Complete the Installation

1. Install the System: Review your selections, then click "Install" to begin the installation process. The installer will copy files and configure your system.

2. Finish and Reboot: Once the installation is complete, you'll be prompted to remove the installation media and reboot your computer. After rebooting, your system should boot into Linux.

Installing Linux on a Virtual Machine

If you prefer to run Linux in a virtual environment, you can use software like VirtualBox or VMware to create a virtual machine (VM). Here's how:

Step 1: Set Up the Virtual Machine

- Install VirtualBox or VMware: Download and install the virtualization software on your host machine.
- Create a New VM:

  - Open the software and select "New" to create a new virtual machine.

  - Name your VM and select the type (Linux) and version (choose the appropriate distribution, e.g., Ubuntu, Debian).

  - Allocate memory (RAM) for the VM. 2 GB is usually sufficient for most distributions.

- Set Up the Virtual Hard Disk:

  - Choose to create a new virtual hard disk.

  - Select the type of disk (VDI, VMDK, etc.) and whether it should be dynamically allocated or fixed-size.

  - Allocate disk space. 20 GB is a good starting point.

Step 2: Install Linux on the VM

- Attach the ISO File: In the VM settings, go to the "Storage" section and attach the downloaded ISO file as a virtual optical disk.
- Start the VM: Start the virtual machine. It will boot from the attached ISO file, and you can follow the same installation steps as for a physical machine.
- Complete the Installation: After installation, you can remove the ISO file from the virtual optical drive and reboot the VM.

Your Linux system will start up in the virtual machine environment.

Installing Linux on a Server

Installing Linux on a server is similar to installing on a desktop or laptop but with some key differences:

Step 1: Choose a Server Distribution

- Ubuntu Server: A popular choice with robust community support.

- CentOS Stream: Known for its stability in enterprise environments.

- Debian: A reliable choice for servers with a focus on free software.

Step 2: Follow the Server-Specific Installation Process

- Boot from Installation Media: As with desktops, boot the server from the USB drive or DVD containing the server distribution.
- Select Server-Specific Options: Server distributions often ask about software packages to install (e.g., LAMP stack, SSH server) during installation.
- Partitioning: Consider setting up separate partitions for `/var`, `/home`, and `/tmp` for better security and performance.
- Create a Root Account: Unlike desktop distributions, server installations often require setting up a root account in addition to a regular user account.
- Network Configuration: Configure network settings, such as assigning a static IP address if required.

- Install and Reboot: Complete the installation and reboot the server. After rebooting, you'll have a command-line interface, ready to configure your server for its intended purpose.

Regardless of the platform, installing Linux is a rewarding experience that opens up a world of possibilities. Whether you're setting up Linux on your personal computer, virtual machine, or server, this guide provides you with the essential steps to get started. Once installed, you'll be ready to explore the powerful and flexible environment that Linux offers.

Post-Installation Configuration

Setting Up Your Linux Environment

Once you've installed Linux, the next crucial step is configuring your environment to suit your needs. Proper post-installation configuration not only enhances the usability and performance of your system but also ensures that your setup is secure and optimized for your specific tasks.

Updating and Upgrading Your System

After installation, it's essential to ensure that your system is up to date with the latest software and security patches.

- Update Package Lists: The first step is to refresh the package lists from the repositories. This ensures you have the latest information about available software.

```bash
sudo apt update
```

- Upgrade Installed Packages: Once the package lists are updated, upgrade the installed packages to their latest versions.

```bash
sudo apt upgrade
```

- Full Upgrade: In some cases, a full upgrade might be necessary to ensure all dependencies and system packages are up to date.

```bash
sudo apt full-upgrade
```

- Remove Unnecessary Packages: Clean up any unused packages that were automatically installed but are no longer needed.

```bash
sudo apt autoremove
```

Installing Essential Software

Depending on your use case, you'll want to install software that will help you work efficiently on your new Linux system.

- Development Tools: If you're planning to develop software, install build-essential packages that include compilers, debuggers, and other necessary tools.

```bash
sudo apt install build-essential
```

- Productivity Software: For day-to-day tasks, consider installing LibreOffice, GIMP, and other productivity applications.

```bash
sudo apt install libreoffice gimp
```

- Web Browser: Most distributions come with a web browser pre-installed, but you can install alternatives like Firefox, Chromium, or Brave.

```bash
sudo apt install firefox
```

- Version Control: Git is a must-have tool for developers to manage code versions.

```bash
sudo apt install git
```

Configuring User Accounts and Permissions

Setting up user accounts and permissions properly is critical for system security.

- Create a New User Account: If you didn't create a non-root user during installation, it's essential to create one now.

```bash
```

```
sudo adduser username
```
```

```

- Grant Sudo Privileges: Add your user to the sudo group to grant administrative privileges.

```bash
sudo usermod -aG sudo username
```
```

```

- Configure SSH Access: For remote access, configure SSH. Start by installing the SSH server.

```bash
sudo apt install openssh-server
```
```

```

- Harden SSH Security: Modify the `/etc/ssh/sshd_config` file to disable root login and change the default SSH port to enhance security.

Customizing the Desktop Environment

If you're using a desktop version of Linux, you can customize the desktop environment to match your workflow.

- Install and Switch Desktop Environments: Depending on your preference, you can install alternative desktop environments like GNOME, KDE, or Xfce.

```bash
sudo apt install kde-plasma-desktop
```

- Change Appearance Settings: Customize the look and feel by changing themes, icons, and fonts through your desktop environment's settings.

- Set Up Workspaces: Configure multiple workspaces to organize your tasks more efficiently. Most desktop environments support multiple virtual desktops.

Setting Up System Backups

Regular backups are crucial to protect your data in case of system failure.

- Install Backup Software: Tools like Timeshift or rsync are popular for setting up system and data backups.

```bash
sudo apt install timeshift
```

- Configure Backup Schedule: Set up automatic backups to an external drive or cloud service at regular intervals.

Configuring Firewall and Security Settings

Securing your Linux environment is essential, especially if your system is connected to the internet.

- Enable Firewall: Most Linux distributions come with `ufw` (Uncomplicated Firewall) pre-installed. Enable and configure it to block unauthorized access.

```bash
sudo ufw enable
sudo ufw allow ssh
```

- Install Antivirus (Optional): While Linux is less prone to viruses, installing an antivirus like ClamAV can add an extra layer of security.

```bash
sudo apt install clamav
```

- Regular System Updates: Ensure that your system is configured to check for updates regularly and apply security patches promptly.

Optimizing System Performance

To get the most out of your Linux system, consider making some performance optimizations.

- Adjust Swappiness: Modify the swappiness value to control how much the system relies on swap space.

```bash
sudo sysctl vm.swappiness=10
```

- Enable TRIM for SSDs: If you're using an SSD, enable TRIM to maintain optimal performance over time.

```bash
sudo systemctl enable fstrim.timer
```

- Manage Startup Applications: Disable unnecessary startup applications to improve boot times.

Configuring Networking

If you're using Linux in a networked environment, proper network configuration is key.

- Set Up Static IP (Optional)**: If your system requires a static IP, configure it through the network manager or by editing `/etc/network/interfaces`.

- Connect to Wi-Fi: Use Network Manager for GUI-based Wi-Fi configuration or `wpa_supplicant` for command-line setup.

- Configure DNS: Set custom DNS servers like Google DNS or OpenDNS for faster and more secure browsing.

Installing Additional Drivers

For optimal hardware performance, ensure all necessary drivers are installed.

- Check for Proprietary Drivers: Some hardware requires proprietary drivers, especially for graphics cards and Wi-Fi adapters. Use the "Additional Drivers" tool in Ubuntu-based distributions.

```bash
sudo ubuntu-drivers autoinstall
```

- Install Printer and Scanner Drivers: If you have peripherals like printers or scanners, install the appropriate drivers through your distribution's package manager or from the manufacturer's website.

After completing these post-installation tasks, your Linux environment should be fully operational, secure, and tailored to your needs. Regular maintenance, such as updating your system and reviewing security settings, will ensure that your Linux system remains stable and secure over time.

Navigating the Linux File System

The Linux file system is organized in a hierarchical structure, with directories and subdirectories forming a tree-like arrangement. Understanding this structure is crucial for effectively navigating, managing, and utilizing a Linux system. This chapter explores the fundamental elements of the Linux directory structure, helping you grasp where files are located, how to access them, and the significance of each directory.

The Root Directory (`/`)

The root directory is the starting point of the Linux file system. All other directories and files stem from this root directory, making it the top-level directory in the hierarchy. Unlike some operating systems where each drive has its own root directory (like C:\ in Windows), Linux has a single root directory for the entire file system.

- System Root (`/`): The `/` directory contains essential system files and directories required for the system to operate.

Key Directories Under Root

Several critical directories are located directly under the root directory. Each serves a specific purpose in the Linux operating system.

- `/bin`: Short for "binary," this directory contains essential user command binaries (executable files) necessary for basic system operations, such as `ls`, `cp`, and `mv`.

- `/sbin`: Similar to `/bin`, but this directory holds system binaries, primarily used by the root user for system administration tasks, like `shutdown` and `fdisk`.

- `/etc`: This directory contains system-wide configuration files and scripts. For example, network configuration files and system services are located here.

- `/home`: This directory houses personal directories for each user on the system. For instance, if your username is `john`, your personal files and settings would be stored in `/home/john`.

- `/root`: The home directory for the root user (the system administrator). It is separate from the `/home` directory to ensure system integrity and security.

- `/var`: Short for "variable," this directory stores files that are expected to grow in size over time, such as logs, caches, and databases. Key subdirectories include `/var/log` for system logs and `/var/www` for web server files.

- `/usr`: This stands for "user" and is a large directory containing user applications and utilities. It is further divided into subdirectories like `/usr/bin` for user commands, `/usr/lib` for libraries, and `/usr/share` for shared data.

- `/lib`: Contains essential shared libraries required by the binaries in `/bin` and `/sbin`. It is analogous to the `System32` folder in Windows.

- `/tmp`: A temporary directory used by the system and applications to store transient files. Files in `/tmp` are often cleared upon reboot.

- `/dev`: The device files directory, containing special files that represent hardware components like hard drives, USB devices, and more. Each device in the system is represented as a file within this directory.

- `/proc`: A virtual directory containing information about running processes and system resources. It's dynamically created by the system and includes directories like `/proc/1234`, where `1234` is the process ID (PID) of a running process.

- `/sys`: Another virtual directory that provides information about the system and hardware, offering a view into the kernel's view of the hardware.

- `/opt`: Stands for "optional" and is used for installing additional software packages that aren't managed by the system's package manager. This directory is often used for commercial or third-party software.

- `/media` and `/mnt`: These directories are used for mounting external storage devices, such as USB drives, CDs, and other filesystems. While `/media` is typically used by the system to auto-mount devices, `/mnt` is used by administrators for manual mounting.

Navigating the Directory Structure

To effectively use the Linux file system, it's essential to know how to navigate between directories using the command line.

- Listing Directory Contents: The `ls` command is used to list files and directories within a directory. For example, `ls /etc` lists the contents of the `/etc` directory.
- Changing Directories: Use the `cd` (change directory) command to navigate between directories. For example, `cd /home/john` would move you to the `john` user's home directory.

- Checking the Current Directory: The `pwd` (print working directory) command displays your current location within the file system.
- Relative vs. Absolute Paths: An absolute path starts from the root directory (e.g., `/home/john/Documents`), while a relative path is based on your current directory (e.g., `Documents/Work` if you're already in `/home/john`).

Permissions and Ownership

Understanding the permissions and ownership of files and directories is crucial for maintaining system security and functionality.

- File Permissions: Linux assigns three types of permissions to each file and directory: read (r), write (w), and execute (x). These permissions are set for three categories of users: the owner, the group, and others.
- Ownership: Each file and directory is owned by a user and a group. Ownership determines who can change the permissions and who has the default permissions.
- Changing Permissions: The `chmod` command is used to change the permissions of a file or directory. For example, `chmod 755 filename` sets the file to be readable and executable by everyone, but writable only by the owner.
- Changing Ownership: The `chown` command changes the ownership of a file or directory. For example, `chown john:staff filename` changes the owner to `john` and the group to `staff`.

Best Practices for File System Management

- Regular Backups: Always back up critical files and configurations, especially before making significant changes.
- Use of Symbolic Links: Create symbolic links for frequently accessed files or directories to avoid duplicating files.
- Avoiding System-Wide Changes as Root: Whenever possible, make changes as a regular user rather than as the root user to avoid accidental system-wide modifications.

Essential File System Commands

Mastering Linux involves getting comfortable with the command line, especially when it comes to managing the file system. In this section, we'll explore some essential file system commands that every Linux user should know. These commands allow you to navigate directories, manipulate files, and understand the structure and content of your system.

Navigating the File System

- `pwd` (Print Working Directory): This command displays the current directory you are working in. It's useful for confirming your location within the directory structure.

  - Example:

    ```bash
    pwd
    ```

    Output:

    ```
    /home/user
    ```

- `cd` (Change Directory): Use `cd` to move between directories. You can specify an absolute path (starting from `/`) or a relative path (based on your current directory).

  - Example (absolute path):

```bash
cd /var/log
```

- Example (relative path):

```bash
cd Documents/Projects
```

- **`ls` (List):** The `ls` command lists the contents of a directory. You can use various options to customize its output, such as `-l` for a detailed list or `-a` to show hidden files.

  - Example:

```bash
ls -l
```

Working with Files and Directories

- `mkdir` (Make Directory): Creates a new directory. You can create multiple directories at once or use the `-p` option to create parent directories as needed.

  - Example:

```bash
```

mkdir new_directory

```
```

- `rmdir` (Remove Directory): Deletes an empty directory. If the directory contains files, you'll need to use `rm -r` to remove it and its contents.

  - Example:

    ```bash
    rmdir old_directory
    ```

- `touch` (Create or Update a File): Creates an empty file or updates the timestamp of an existing file.

  - Example:

    ```bash
    touch newfile.txt
    ```

- `cp` (Copy): Copies files or directories. Use the `-r` option to copy directories recursively.

  - Example (copying a file):

    ```bash
```

cp file1.txt /path/to/destination/
```

  - Example (copying a directory):

    ```bash

    cp -r dir1 /path/to/destination/
    ```


- `mv` (Move or Rename): Moves files or directories to a new
location or renames them.

  - Example (moving a file):

    ```bash

    mv file1.txt /path/to/destination/
    ```

  - Example (renaming a file):

    ```bash

    mv oldname.txt newname.txt
    ```


- `rm` (Remove): Deletes files or directories. Use `-r` to remove
directories and their contents recursively, and `-f` to force the
deletion without prompting.

  - Example (removing a file):
    ```

```bash
rm file1.txt
```

- Example (removing a directory):

```bash
rm -r dir1
```

Viewing and Editing Files

- `cat` (Concatenate): Displays the contents of a file. It's useful for viewing short files or combining multiple files into one.

  - Example:

  ```bash
  cat file1.txt
  ```

- `more` and `less` (View File Content): `more` displays file contents one screen at a time, while `less` allows you to scroll up and down.

  - Example:

  ```bash
  less file1.txt
  ```

```
```

- `head` and `tail` (View Beginning/End of Files): `head` shows the first 10 lines of a file, while `tail` shows the last 10 lines. You can adjust the number of lines with the `-n` option.

  - Example (viewing the first 10 lines):

    ```bash
    head file1.txt
    ```

  - Example (viewing the last 10 lines):

    ```bash
    tail file1.txt
    ```

- `nano`, `vi`, `vim` (Text Editors): These are command-line text editors. `nano` is beginner-friendly, while `vi` and `vim` offer powerful editing capabilities.

  - Example (opening a file in nano):

    ```bash
    nano file1.txt
    ```

Managing File Permissions and Ownership

- `chmod` (Change Mode): Changes the permissions of a file or directory. Permissions are defined by three groups: owner, group, and others. You can set read (`r`), write (`w`), and execute (`x`) permissions using symbolic (e.g., `u+x`) or numeric (e.g., `755`) notation.

  - Example (making a file executable):

    ```bash
    chmod +x script.sh
    ```

- `chown` (Change Ownership): Changes the ownership of a file or directory. You can change both the owner and the group.

  - Example:

    ```bash
    chown user:group file1.txt
    ```

- `chgrp` (Change Group): Changes the group ownership of a file or directory.

  - Example:

    ```bash
    chgrp groupname file1.txt
    ```

```
```

Searching and Finding Files

- `find` (Find Files and Directories): Searches for files and directories based on various criteria like name, size, or modification time.

  - Example (finding a file by name):

    ```bash
    find / -name "file1.txt"
    ```

- `grep` (Search Within Files): Searches for a specific pattern within files. You can use regular expressions for more complex searches.

  - Example (searching for a word in a file):

    ```bash
    grep "search_term" file1.txt
    ```

- `locate` (Locate Files): Quickly finds files by name. The `locate` command relies on a database that is periodically updated, making it faster but potentially outdated compared to `find`.

  - Example:

```bash
locate file1.txt
```

Disk Usage and Monitoring

- `df` (Disk Free): Reports the amount of disk space used and available on all mounted filesystems.

  - Example:

  ```bash
  df -h
  ```

- `du` (Disk Usage): Estimates file and directory space usage. You can use `-h` for human-readable format and `-s` for summary.

  - Example:

  ```bash
  du -sh /home/user/
  ```

- `top` and `htop` (Process Monitoring): Displays the system's running processes and resource usage in real-time. `htop` is a more user-friendly version of `top` with additional features.

  - Example (using top):

    ```bash
    top
    ```

Archiving and Compressing Files

- `tar` (Tape Archive): Archives multiple files into a single file, often used with compression options like `-z` for gzip or `-j` for bzip2.

  - Example (creating a compressed archive):

    ```bash
    tar -czvf archive.tar.gz /path/to/directory
    ```

- `gzip` and `gunzip` (Compression/Decompression): Compresses or decompresses files using the gzip algorithm.

  - Example (compressing a file):

    ```bash
    gzip file1.txt
    ```

```
```

- Example (decompressing a file):

  ```bash
  gunzip file1.txt.gz
  ```


- `zip` and `unzip` (ZIP Compression): Compresses or decompresses files using the ZIP format, which is widely used across different operating systems.

  - Example (creating a zip file):

    ```bash
    zip archive.zip file1.txt file2.txt
    ```

  - Example (extracting a zip file):

    ```bash
    unzip archive.zip
    ```

File Permissions and Ownership

In Linux, file permissions and ownership are fundamental concepts that ensure the security and integrity of files and directories. Understanding how to manage these permissions is crucial for both system administrators and regular users, as it helps control who can read, write, or execute a file. This section covers the basics of file permissions, how to change them, and the role of ownership in Linux.

Understanding File Permissions

Linux uses a simple yet powerful permission model that includes three types of permissions:

- Read (`r`): Allows viewing the contents of a file or listing the contents of a directory.
- Write (`w`): Allows modifying the contents of a file or creating/deleting files in a directory.
- Execute (`x`): Allows executing a file (if it's a script or binary) or accessing a directory.

These permissions are applied to three categories of users:

- Owner (User): The user who created the file or directory.

- Group: A collection of users who share the same permissions for the file or directory.

- Others: All other users who have access to the system.

Permissions are represented using a three-part notation, such as `rwxr-xr--`. This notation shows the permissions for the owner, group, and others in that order.

Example:

- `rwx` (for the owner) means the owner has read, write, and execute permissions.

- `r-x` (for the group) means the group has read and execute permissions, but not write permissions.

- `r--` (for others) means others have read-only access.

Viewing File Permissions

To view the permissions of a file or directory, use the `ls -l` command. This command lists files and directories in a long format, showing their permissions, ownership, and other details.

Example:
```bash
ls -l filename.txt
```

Output:
```
-rw-r--r-- 1 user group 1045 Aug 21 12:34 filename.txt
```

```
```

In this example:

- `-rw-r--r--`: Indicates the permissions (read and write for the owner, read-only for the group, and others).
- `user`: Indicates the owner of the file.
- `group`: Indicates the group that owns the file.
- `1045`: Indicates the file size in bytes.
- `Aug 21 12:34`: Indicates the last modified date and time.
- `filename.txt`: Indicates the file name.

Changing File Permissions with `chmod`

The `chmod` command is used to change the permissions of a file or directory. Permissions can be set using symbolic or numeric (octal) notation.

- Symbolic Notation: This method uses characters (`r`, `w`, `x`) to add or remove permissions.

Example:

- Grant execute permission to the owner:

  ```bash

  chmod u+x filename.txt

  ```

- Remove write permission from the group:

```bash
chmod g-w filename.txt
```

Numeric Notation: This method uses a three-digit octal number to set permissions. Each digit represents the permissions for the owner, group, and others, respectively.

The octal values are:

- `4`: Read (`r`)

- `2`: Write (`w`)

- `1`: Execute (`x`)

Example:

- Set permissions to `rwxr-xr--` (Owner: `7` (`rwx`), Group: `5` (`r-x`), Others: `4` (`r--`)):

```bash
chmod 754 filename.txt
```

Changing File Ownership with `chown`

The `chown` command is used to change the ownership of a file or directory. This includes changing both the owner and the group associated with the file.

- Changing the Owner: You can assign a new owner to a file by specifying the username.

Example:

```bash
chown newuser filename.txt
```

- Changing the Group: You can change the group ownership by specifying the group name.

Example:

```bash
chown :newgroup filename.txt
```

- Changing Both Owner and Group: You can change both the owner and group simultaneously.

Example:

```bash
chown newuser:newgroup filename.txt
```

Using `chgrp` to Change Group Ownership

The `chgrp` command is specifically used to change the group ownership of a file or directory.

Example:

```bash
chgrp newgroup filename.txt
```

This command changes the group ownership of `filename.txt` to `newgroup`.

Special Permissions: SUID, SGID, and Sticky Bit

Linux also offers special permissions that provide additional control over how files and directories are accessed and modified:

- SUID (Set User ID): When applied to an executable file, this permission allows users to run the file with the permissions of the file owner.

  - Example: Setting SUID on a file:

  ```bash
  chmod u+s filename
  ```

- SGID (Set Group ID): When applied to a directory, new files created within that directory inherit the group ownership of the directory.

  - Example: Setting SGID on a directory:

  ```bash
  chmod g+s directoryname
  ```

- Sticky Bit: When applied to a directory, the sticky bit ensures that only the file owner (or the root user) can delete or modify the files within that directory.

  - Example: Setting the sticky bit on a directory:

  ```bash
  chmod +t directoryname
  ```

Practical Examples

Here are some practical examples of changing file permissions and ownership:

- Making a Script Executable: If you write a script and want to execute it, you need to add the execute permission.

```bash
chmod +x script.sh
```

- Restricting Access to a File: Suppose you have a sensitive file that you want only the owner to read and write, with no permissions for others.

```bash
chmod 600 sensitivefile.txt
```

- Changing Ownership of a Project Directory: You might want to transfer ownership of a directory and its contents to another user.

```bash
chown -R newuser:newgroup /path/to/project
```

Linux Command Line Basics

Terminal and Shell

The terminal and shell are at the heart of Linux, providing a powerful interface for interacting with the system. While modern Linux distributions come with graphical user interfaces (GUIs), the terminal offers unmatched control, flexibility, and efficiency, making it a vital tool for both beginners and experienced users.

What is the Terminal?

The terminal, also known as the command line interface (CLI), is a text-based interface that allows users to interact directly with the operating system by typing commands. Unlike a graphical interface, which relies on clicking and visual cues, the terminal requires you to input commands using a keyboard. The terminal is often accessed through terminal emulators, software that replicates the functionality of traditional physical terminals on modern systems.

Examples of terminal emulators include:

* GNOME Terminal
* Konsole** (KDE)
* Xfce Terminal
* Terminator

What is a Shell?

The shell is a command interpreter that processes the commands you enter in the terminal. It acts as an intermediary between the user and the operating system, interpreting your input and executing corresponding system calls or scripts.

Several types of shells are available in Linux, each with unique features:

- Bash (Bourne Again Shell): The most common shell in Linux, known for its ease of use and extensive features.
- Zsh (Z Shell): Offers powerful customization and scripting capabilities, often preferred by advanced users.
- Fish (Friendly Interactive Shell): Known for its user-friendly syntax and interactive features.
- Tcsh/Csh (TENEX C Shell/C Shell): C shell variants, with syntax influenced by the C programming language.

Most Linux distributions come with Bash as the default shell, but users can switch to a different shell if desired.

Navigating the Terminal

Once you open the terminal, you'll be greeted with a prompt. The prompt is a symbol or set of symbols that indicate the terminal is ready to accept commands. It usually contains information like the current user, hostname, and working directory.

Example of a typical Bash prompt:

```bash
```

```
username@hostname:~$
```


- `username`: Your current user name.

- `hostname`: The name of your computer or system.

- `~`: Represents your home directory.

- `$`: Indicates that you are a regular user (not a superuser).

Basic Shell Commands

Here are some fundamental commands to get you started:

- `pwd` (Print Working Directory): Displays the current directory you are in.

```bash
pwd
```


- `ls` (List Directory Contents): Lists the files and directories in the current directory.

```bash
ls
```

- Use `ls -l` for a detailed list with permissions, file sizes, and timestamps.

- Use `ls -a` to include hidden files (files starting with a dot).

- `cd` (Change Directory): Changes your current directory to another one.

```bash
cd /path/to/directory
```

- `cd ~` or simply `cd` takes you to your home directory.

- `cd ..` moves you up one directory level.

- `mkdir` (Make Directory): Creates a new directory.

```bash
mkdir new_directory
```


- `rmdir` (Remove Directory): Deletes an empty directory.

```bash
rmdir empty_directory
```

- `rm` (Remove File or Directory): Removes files or directories.

```bash
rm filename
```

  - Use `rm -r` to remove a directory and its contents recursively.

- `touch` (Create an Empty File): Creates an empty file or updates the timestamp of an existing file.

```bash
touch newfile.txt
```

- `cp` (Copy Files or Directories): Copies files or directories from one location to another.

```bash
cp source_file destination
```

- `mv` (Move or Rename Files or Directories): Moves or renames files or directories.

```bash
mv oldname newname
```

```
```

- To move a file to another directory:

  ```bash

  mv filename /path/to/directory

  ```


- `cat` (Concatenate and Display Files): Displays the contents of a file.

  ```bash

  cat filename.txt

  ```


- `less` and `more`: Scroll through the contents of a file one screen at a time.

  ```bash

  less filename.txt

  ```


- `man` (Manual Pages): Displays the manual or help page for a command.

  ```bash

  man command_name
  ```

```
```

Command Line Tips and Tricks

- Tab Completion: When typing a command or file path, pressing `Tab` can auto-complete the text or provide suggestions.
- Command History: Use the up and down arrow keys to scroll through previously executed commands.

- `Ctrl + C`: Interrupts or stops the current command.

- `Ctrl + L`: Clears the terminal screen.

Understanding Shell Scripts

Shell scripts are text files containing a sequence of commands that are executed by the shell. Scripts allow users to automate repetitive tasks or perform complex operations with a single command.

A simple shell script example:

```bash
#!/bin/bash

# This is a comment

echo "Hello, World!"
```

- `#!/bin/bash`: Indicates that the script should be run in the Bash shell.

- `echo "Hello, World!"`: Outputs the text "Hello, World!" to the terminal.

To run the script:

1. Save it as `myscript.sh`.

2. Make it executable with `chmod +x myscript.sh`.

3. Execute it with `./myscript.sh`.

Commonly Used Linux Commands

Mastering Linux commands is key to effectively managing and interacting with a Linux system. These commands allow you to perform a wide range of tasks, from managing files to monitoring system performance. Below is a list of commonly used Linux commands that every user should know.

File and Directory Management

- `ls` (List Directory Contents):

  - Lists files and directories in the current directory.

- Variants:

  - `ls -l`: Detailed list including permissions, sizes, and timestamps.

    - `ls -a`: Lists all files, including hidden ones.

- `cd` (Change Directory):

  - Changes the current directory.

    ```bash
    cd /path/to/directory
    ```

- `pwd` (Print Working Directory):

- Displays the full path of the current directory.

```bash
pwd
```

- `mkdir` (Make Directory):
  - Creates a new directory.

```bash
mkdir new_directory
```

- `rmdir` (Remove Directory):
  - Deletes an empty directory.

```bash
rmdir directory_name
```

- `rm` (Remove Files or Directories):
  - Deletes files or directories.

```bash
rm filename
```

```
```

- Use `rm -r` to remove directories and their contents recursively.

• `cp` (Copy Files or Directories):

  - Copies files or directories.

    ```bash

    cp source_file destination

    ```


• `mv` (Move or Rename Files or Directories):

  - Moves or renames files or directories.

    ```bash

    mv oldname newname

    ```


• `touch` (Create or Update Files):

  - Creates an empty file or updates the timestamp of an existing file.

    ```bash

    touch filename

    ```

- `find` (Search for Files or Directories):

  - Searches for files or directories in a directory hierarchy.

    ```bash
    find /path -name filename
    ```

File Viewing and Editing

- `cat` (Concatenate and Display Files):

  - Displays the contents of a file.

    ```bash
    cat filename.txt
    ```

- `more` and `less`:

  - Scroll through a file one screen at a time.

    ```bash
    less filename.txt
    ```

- `head` and `tail`:

- `head`: Displays the first 10 lines of a file.

```bash
head filename.txt
```

- `tail`: Displays the last 10 lines of a file.

```bash
tail filename.txt
```

- `nano`, `vi`, and `vim`:

  - Text editors for creating or modifying files.

  - `nano` is user-friendly, while `vi` and `vim` are more powerful but have steeper learning curves.

```bash
nano filename.txt
vi filename.txt
vim filename.txt
```

System Information and Monitoring

- `uname` (Unix Name):

- Displays system information.

```bash
uname -a
```

- `top` and `htop`:

  - `top`: Displays real-time system processes and resource usage.

```bash
top
```

  - `htop`: A more user-friendly version of `top` with enhanced features.

- `df` (Disk Free):

  - Displays disk space usage for file systems.

```bash
df -h
```

- `du` (Disk Usage):

  - Estimates file space usage.

```bash
du -sh /path/to/directory
```

- `free`:
  - Displays memory usage.
  ```bash
  free -h
  ```

- `ps` (Process Status):
  - Lists current running processes.
  ```bash
  ps aux
  ```

- `kill`:
  - Terminates a process by its PID.
  ```bash
  kill PID
  ```

- `uptime`:

  - Shows how long the system has been running.

    ```bash
    uptime
    ```

Networking Commands

- `ping`:

  - Tests connectivity to a network host.

    ```bash
    ping www.example.com
    ```
    `

- `ifconfig` or `ip a`:

  - Displays network interface information.

    ```bash
    ifconfig
    ip a
    ```

- `netstat`:

  - Displays network connections, routing tables, and interface statistics.

  ```bash
  netstat -tuln
  ```

- `wget` and `curl`:

  - `wget`: Downloads files from the web.

  ```bash
  wget http://example.com/file.txt
  ```

  - `curl`: Transfers data to or from a server, supporting various protocols.

  ```bash
  curl -O http://example.com/file.txt
  ```

- `ssh`:

  - Securely connects to a remote server over the network.

  ```bash
  ssh user@remote_host
  ```

```
```

Permissions and Ownership

- `chmod` (Change Mode):

  - Changes file or directory permissions.

  ```bash
  chmod 755 filename
  ```

- `chown` (Change Ownership):

  - Changes the ownership of a file or directory.

  ```bash
  chown user:group filename
  ```

- `umask`:

  - Sets default permissions for new files and directories.

  ```bash
  umask 022
  ```

Package Management

- `apt` (Advanced Package Tool) (Debian/Ubuntu-based systems):

  - Installs, updates, and removes packages.

  ```bash
  sudo apt update

  sudo apt install package_name
  ```

- `yum` or `dnf` (Red Hat/CentOS/Fedora):

  - Manages packages on Red Hat-based systems.

  ```bash
  sudo yum install package_name

  sudo dnf install package_name
  ```

- `pacman` (Arch Linux):

  - Manages packages on Arch-based systems.

  ```bash
  sudo pacman -S package_name
  ```

Archiving and Compression

- `tar`:

  - Archives multiple files into a single file and optionally compresses it.

  ```bash
  tar -cvf archive.tar file1 file2 file3
  tar -xvf archive.tar
  ```

- `gzip` and `gunzip`:
  - Compresses and decompresses files using the gzip algorithm.

  ```bash
  gzip filename
  gunzip filename.gz
  ```

- `zip` and `unzip`:
  - Compresses and decompresses files using the zip algorithm.

  ```bash
  zip archive.zip file1 file2
  ```

unzip archive.zip
```

## Miscellaneous Commands

- `alias`:
  - Creates shortcuts for commands.
    ```bash
    alias ll='ls -la'
    ```

- `whoami`:
  - Displays the current logged-in user.
    ```bash
    whoami
    ```

- `history`:
  - Shows the history of commands entered in the terminal.
    ```bash
    history
    ```
    ```

- `date`:

  - Displays or sets the system date and time.

    ```bash
    date
    ```

- `reboot` and `shutdown`:

  - Reboots or shuts down the system.

    ```bash
    sudo reboot
    sudo shutdown -h now
    ```

These commands form the foundation of Linux system administration and everyday tasks. Familiarizing yourself with them will enhance your ability to navigate, manage, and troubleshoot Linux systems effectively. As you continue to explore and use these commands, you'll develop a deeper understanding of the power and flexibility that the Linux command line offers.

SCRIPTING BASICS: AUTOMATING TASKS WITH SHELL SCRIPTS

Shell scripting is a powerful tool in Linux, allowing users to automate repetitive tasks, manage system processes, and streamline workflows. A shell script is simply a file containing a series of commands that are executed sequentially by the shell.

A shell script is a text file containing a series of commands. When executed, these commands are run in the order they appear in the file, automating tasks that would otherwise have to be performed manually. Shell scripts are typically written using a text editor and saved with a `.sh` extension.

Creating Your First Shell Script

Let's walk through the process of creating a basic shell script.

1. Open a text editor:

   - Use any text editor you prefer, such as `nano`, `vi`, or `vim`.

   - For example:

   ```bash
   nano first_script.sh
   ```

2. Write your script:

- Start with the shebang (`#!/bin/bash`), which tells the system that the script should be run in the Bash shell.

- Add a series of commands you want to automate.

- Example script:

```bash
#!/bin/bash
echo "Hello, World!"
date
```

3. Save and close the script:

- Save the file and exit the text editor.

4. Make the script executable:

- Before running the script, you need to make it executable.

```bash
chmod +x first_script.sh
```

5. Run the script:

- Execute your script by typing `./` followed by the script name.

```bash
./first_script.sh
```

- You should see the output of the `echo` and `date` commands.

Script Structure and Syntax

Understanding the basic structure and syntax of shell scripts is crucial for writing effective scripts.

Shebang (`#!/bin/bash`):

 - This line specifies the interpreter to be used to execute the script. While Bash is the most common shell, others like `#!/bin/sh` or `#!/usr/bin/env bash` can be used.

Comments (`#`):

 - Comments are lines that are not executed. They start with `#` and are used to document the script.

```bash
# This is a comment
```

Variables:

- Variables store values that can be reused throughout the script.

```bash
greeting="Hello"
echo $greeting
```

Control Structures:

- Conditional Statements:

```bash
if [ condition ]
then
  # commands
fi
```

- **Loops**:

  - **For loop**:

```bash
for i in 1 2 3
do
  echo $i
```

done

```
```

- **While loop**:

```bash
while [ condition ]

do

  # commands

done
```

Practical Examples of Shell Scripts

Here are some practical examples where shell scripting can be applied:

Backup Script:

- Automate the process of backing up important files.

```bash
#!/bin/bash

tar -czf /backup/my_backup_$(date +%F).tar.gz /home/user/documents

echo "Backup completed."
```

System Monitoring Script:

- Monitor system resources like CPU and memory usage.

```bash
#!/bin/bash
echo "System Information for $(hostname)"
echo "------------------------------"
echo "Date: $(date)"
echo "Uptime: $(uptime)"
echo "Memory Usage:"
free -h
echo "Disk Usage:"
df -h
```

Automated Update Script:

- Automatically update the system's packages.

```bash
#!/bin/bash
sudo apt update && sudo apt upgrade -y
echo "System updated."
```

Best Practices for Writing Shell Scripts

Use Comments:

  - Document your code with comments to make it easier to understand and maintain.

Test Scripts Incrementally:

  - Test small parts of your script as you write it to catch errors early.

Error Handling:

  - Incorporate error handling to manage unexpected situations.

```bash
if [ $? -ne 0 ]; then
  echo "Error occurred"
  exit 1
fi
```

Avoid Hard-Coding Values:

  - Use variables to store values instead of hard-coding them.

Use Meaningful Names:

 - Use descriptive names for variables and functions to enhance readability.

Managing Software on Linux

Package management systems are essential tools in Linux that simplify the process of installing, updating, and removing software. They automate the handling of software dependencies, ensuring that all necessary components are installed or removed alongside the main package. Here's a closer look at some of the most widely used package management systems in Linux:

APT (Advanced Package Tool)

APT is the package management system used in Debian-based distributions like Ubuntu, Debian, and Linux Mint. It is known for its ease of use and extensive repository of software packages.

Common Commands:

- `sudo apt-get install package_name`: Installs a package.

- `sudo apt-get update`: Updates the list of available packages.

- `sudo apt-get upgrade`: Upgrades all installed packages to their latest versions.

- `sudo apt-get remove package_name`: Removes a package.

Features:

- Dependency Resolution**: Automatically handles dependencies, ensuring all required libraries and tools are installed.
- Repositories**: APT pulls software from official and third-party repositories, offering a vast range of applications.

YUM (Yellowdog Updater, Modified)

YUM is used in Red Hat-based distributions like CentOS and Fedora. It was designed to manage RPM packages and is known for its ability to work with a network of repositories.

Common Commands:

- `sudo yum install package_name`: Installs a package.

- `sudo yum update`: Updates all installed packages.

- `sudo yum remove package_name`: Removes a package.

Features:

- Repository Management: YUM can work with multiple repositories, making it flexible for enterprise environments.
- Group Installations: Allows the installation of groups of related packages, such as `sudo yum groupinstall "Development Tools"`.

DNF (Dandified YUM)

DNF is the next-generation version of YUM, used in newer Red Hat-based distributions like Fedora and CentOS. It offers better performance and more reliable dependency management.

Common Commands:

- `sudo dnf install package_name`: Installs a package.

- `sudo dnf update`: Updates all installed packages.

- `sudo dnf remove package_name`: Removes a package.

Features

- Improved Dependency Handling: DNF provides more accurate and faster resolution of package dependencies.
- Plugin Support: Offers a wide range of plugins to extend its functionality, such as automatic cleanup of old kernels.

Pacman

Pacman is the package manager for Arch Linux and its derivatives. It is known for its simplicity and speed, making it a favorite among Arch users.

Common Commands:

- `sudo pacman -S package_name`: Installs a package.

- `sudo pacman -Syu`: Synchronizes the package databases and upgrades all packages.

- `sudo pacman -R package_name`: Removes a package.

Features:

- Binary Package Management: Pacman handles binary packages, ensuring that users can quickly install and update software.
- Custom Repositories: Users can easily add and manage custom repositories, offering flexibility in package sourcing.

Zypper

Zypper is the package manager for openSUSE and SUSE Linux Enterprise. It is known for its powerful command-line interface and robust dependency resolution.

Common Commands:

- `sudo zypper install package_name`: Installs a package.

- `sudo zypper update`: Updates all installed packages.

- `sudo zypper remove package_name`: Removes a package.

Features:

- Dependency Management: Like other package managers, Zypper handles dependencies automatically.
- Pattern Installations: Zypper allows the installation of patterns, which are predefined groups of packages for specific tasks, such as `sudo zypper install -t pattern devel_basis` for development tools.

Installing, Updating, and Removing Software

Efficient software management in Linux is crucial for maintaining system stability and performance. This involves not only installing, updating, and removing software but also managing dependencies and repositories effectively.

Installing Software

Installing software on Linux typically involves using a package manager that handles the retrieval and installation of software packages from repositories.

Process:

Using a Package Manager:

- For Debian-based systems (e.g., Ubuntu):

    - Command: `sudo apt-get install package_name`

- For Red Hat-based systems (e.g., CentOS, Fedora):

    - Command: `sudo yum install package_name` or `sudo dnf install package_name`

- For Arch-based systems (e.g., Arch Linux, Manjaro):

    - Command: `sudo pacman -S package_name`

- For SUSE-based systems (e.g., openSUSE):

    - Command: `sudo zypper install package_name`

Manual Installation:

Sometimes, software needs to be installed manually, especially if it's not available in standard repositories. This can involve downloading a `.deb`, `.rpm`, or source code tarball and manually installing it using commands like `dpkg`, `rpm`, or `make`.

Updating Software

Regularly updating software is essential to keep the system secure and stable. Updates may include security patches, bug fixes, and new features.

Process:

System-Wide Update:

- Debian-based systems:

    - Command: `sudo apt-get update` (refreshes the package list)

    - Command: `sudo apt-get upgrade` (upgrades all installed packages)

- Red Hat-based systems:

    - Command: `sudo yum update` or `sudo dnf update`

- Arch-based systems:

    - Command: `sudo pacman -Syu`

- SUSE-based systems:

    - Command: `sudo zypper update`

Selective Updating:

Sometimes, you may want to update only specific packages. This can be done by specifying the package name after the update command, e.g., `sudo apt-get install --only-upgrade package_name`.

Removing Software

Removing unnecessary or obsolete software helps free up disk space and reduces potential security vulnerabilities.

Process:

Uninstalling a Package:

* Debian-based systems:

    - Command: `sudo apt-get remove package_name`

* Red Hat-based systems:

    - Command: `sudo yum remove package_name` or `sudo dnf remove package_name`

* Arch-based systems:

    - Command: `sudo pacman -R package_name`

* SUSE-based systems:

    - Command: `sudo zypper remove package_name`

Complete Removal:

To remove a package along with its configuration files:

    - Debian-based systems: `sudo apt-get purge package_name`

    - Arch-based systems: `sudo pacman -Rns package_name`

Cleaning Up:

After removing packages, you can clean up unused dependencies and residual files using:

    - Debian-based systems: `sudo apt-get autoremove`

    - Red Hat-based systems: `sudo dnf autoremove`

    - Arch-based systems: `sudo pacman -Rns $(pacman -Qdtq)`

Managing Dependencies

Dependencies are additional packages that a software package requires to function correctly. Managing dependencies ensures that all necessary components are installed and maintained.

- Automatic Dependency Handling:

  - Package managers like APT, YUM, DNF, and Pacman automatically handle dependencies during installation, ensuring that all required libraries and tools are installed.

- Resolving Dependency Issues:

  - If a package manager reports missing or conflicting dependencies, commands like `sudo apt-get -f install` (for fixing broken dependencies in APT) can resolve these issues.

- For more complex dependency issues, manually installing or removing specific packages might be necessary.

Managing Repositories

- Repositories are servers that store software packages. Managing repositories effectively ensures access to the latest software and updates.

Adding Repositories:

- To add a new repository to your system, you typically need to edit the repository configuration files or use package manager commands:

Debian-based systems:

   - Command: `sudo add-apt-repository ppa:repository_name`

   - After adding, always run `sudo apt-get update`.

Red Hat-based systems:

   - Repositories are often managed via `.repo` files in `/etc/yum.repos.d/` or `/etc/yum.repos.d/` for DNF.

   - Use `sudo yum-config-manager --add-repo URL` or `sudo dnf config-manager --add-repo URL`.

Removing Repositories:

- If you need to remove a repository, you can either delete the corresponding `.repo` file or use the package manager's configuration tool.

Priority and Pinning:

- Some systems allow you to set priority levels for repositories to control which repository's package version is preferred.

User and Group Management

User and group management is a fundamental aspect of Linux system administration, allowing for organized and secure control over who can access and modify system resources. This chapter covers the essential tasks involved in creating and managing users and groups on a Linux system.

Understanding Users and Groups

Users:

In Linux, each user has a unique account that allows them to log in and interact with the system. User accounts are identified by a unique username and user ID (UID).

- Root User: The root user is the superuser with unrestricted access to all commands and files on the system. It is the most powerful account and should be used with caution.

Groups:

Groups are collections of users that can be managed as a single entity. Each group has a unique name and group ID (GID). Users can be members of multiple groups, and group membership determines access permissions to files and resources.

- Primary Group: A user's primary group is the default group assigned to files they create.
- Secondary Groups: These are additional groups a user belongs to, providing further permissions.

Creating Users

Command Overview:

Users are created using the `useradd` command, which sets up a new user account along with a home directory and other necessary configurations.

Basic User Creation:

  - Command: `sudo useradd username`

    - This creates a new user with the specified username.

  - Setting a Password:

    - Command: `sudo passwd username`

    - The `passwd` command sets or changes the password for the specified user.

Creating a User with Specific Options:

  - Home Directory:

    - Command: `sudo useradd -m -d /home/custom_dir username`

    - The `-m` option creates a home directory, and the `-d` option specifies a custom home directory path.

Shell:

    - Command: `sudo useradd -s /bin/bash username`

    - The `-s` option sets the default shell for the user.

- Custom UID:

  - Command: `sudo useradd -u 1001 username`

  - The `-u` option assigns a custom user ID to the new user.

Managing Users

- Modifying User Accounts:

  - Change Username:

    - Command: `sudo usermod -l new_username old_username`

    - The `usermod` command with the `-l` option changes the username.

- Change Home Directory:

    - Command: `sudo usermod -d /new/home/directory username`

    - The `-d` option changes the user's home directory.

 - Add User to a Group:

    - Command: `sudo usermod -aG groupname username`

    - The `-aG` option adds the user to a group without affecting their other group memberships.

- Deleting Users:

  - Remove a User:

- Command: `sudo userdel username`

  - The `userdel` command removes a user account but leaves the home directory intact.

- Remove User and Home Directory**:

  - Command: `sudo userdel -r username`

  - The `-r` option deletes the user account and the home directory.

Creating and Managing Groups

- Creating Groups:

  - Command: `sudo groupadd groupname`

  - The `groupadd` command creates a new group with the specified name.

- Managing Group Membership:

  - Add a User to a Group:

    - Command: `sudo usermod -aG groupname username`

  - This command adds the specified user to the group without removing them from other groups.

- List Group Memberships:

- Command: `groups username`

- This command lists all the groups a user belongs to.

- Modifying Groups:

  - Change Group Name:

    - Command: `sudo groupmod -n new_groupname old_groupname`

    - The `groupmod` command with the `-n` option changes the group's name.

- Delete a Group:

    - Command: `sudo groupdel groupname`

    - The `groupdel` command removes the specified group.

Setting Permissions and Ownership

- File Ownership:

  - Every file in Linux is associated with an owner (user) and a group. Managing ownership is essential for controlling access to files.

  - Change File Ownership:

    - Command: `sudo chown username:groupname filename`

    - The `chown` command changes the owner and group of a file.

- File Permissions:

  - Permissions determine who can read, write, or execute a file. These can be set using the `chmod` command.

  - Change Permissions:

    - Command: `chmod 755 filename`

    - The `chmod` command changes the permissions, where `755` is a common permission setting allowing the owner full control and others to read and execute.

Best Practices for User Security and Account Management

Effective user and group management is crucial for maintaining the security and stability of a Linux system. Implementing best practices ensures that users have appropriate access rights and that system resources are protected from unauthorized use. This section outlines key strategies for managing user accounts securely and efficiently.

Principle of Least Privilege

Description: Users should be given only the permissions necessary to perform their job functions and no more. This minimizes the risk of accidental or malicious actions affecting the system.

Implementation:

- Create separate user accounts for different roles with specific permissions.
- Regularly review and update user privileges to ensure they align with current job responsibilities.
- Use groups to assign permissions to collections of users rather than managing individual permissions.

Regular Account Audits

Description: Periodically review user accounts and group memberships to ensure they are accurate and up-to-date.

Implementation:

- Audit User Accounts:

  - Use commands like `getent passwd` to list all users and verify their activity.

  - Review `/etc/passwd` and `/etc/group` files for discrepancies.

- Review Access Logs:

  - Check logs for unusual login attempts or unauthorized access.

  - Use tools like `last` and `lastlog` to track login activity.

Enforcing Strong Password Policies

Description: Require users to create strong passwords to reduce the risk of unauthorized access.

Implementation:

- Set Password Expiry:

  - Use `chage` to set password expiration dates and enforce regular password changes.

  - Command: `sudo chage -M 90 username` (forces password change every 90 days).

- Password Complexity:

  - Configure password policies in `/etc/login.defs` to enforce complexity rules (e.g., minimum length, character types).

- Use PAM (Pluggable Authentication Modules) to apply additional password policies.

Managing User Access Rights

Description: Carefully manage access rights to files and directories to ensure users have appropriate permissions.

Implementation:

- File Permissions:

  - Set file permissions using `chmod` to control access (e.g., `chmod 750 file` for read, write, and execute permissions for owner and read/execute for group).

- Directory Access:

  - Use access control lists (ACLs) for more granular permission settings, where needed.

  - Command: `setfacl -m u:username:rwx directory` (grants specific user permissions on a directory).

Disabling Inactive Accounts

Description: Disable or remove accounts that are no longer in use to reduce the attack surface.

Implementation:

- Disable Accounts:

  - Use `usermod` to lock accounts that are no longer needed.

- Command: `sudo usermod -L username` (locks the user account).

- **Delete Accounts:**

  - Remove accounts that are permanently inactive.

  - Command: `sudo userdel username` (delete user account, optionally with `-r` to remove home directory).

Implementing Two-Factor Authentication (2FA)

Description: Enhance security by requiring a second form of authentication in addition to the password.

Implementation:

- **Install 2FA Tools:**

  - Use tools like `Google Authenticator` or `Authy` for 2FA.

  - Follow the documentation to configure 2FA for user accounts.

- **Enforce 2FA:**

  - Integrate 2FA with PAM modules to enforce multi-factor authentication at login.

Monitoring and Logging

Description: Continuously monitor user activity and maintain logs to detect and respond to suspicious behavior.

Implementation:

- System Logs:

  - Regularly check logs in `/var/log` (e.g., `auth.log`, `secure`) for unauthorized access attempts.

- Audit Tools:

  - Use tools like `auditd` to track and log system changes.

  - Configure audit rules to monitor specific events or changes.

Educating Users

Provide training and guidance to users on best security practices and the importance of safeguarding their accounts.

Implementation:

- Security Training:

  - Offer regular training sessions on secure password practices, recognizing phishing attempts, and other security topics.

- Security Policies:

  - Develop and distribute clear security policies and guidelines for users to follow.

By adhering to these best practices for user and group management, administrators can ensure a more secure and manageable Linux environment. Implementing the principle of least privilege, conducting regular audits, enforcing strong password policies, and using advanced security measures such as two-factor authentication help mitigate risks and maintain system integrity. Continuous monitoring, user education, and careful management of access rights are crucial for protecting sensitive data and maintaining the overall health of the system.

Process and System Monitoring

Effective management of processes and system resources is critical for maintaining the stability and performance of a Linux system. Understanding how to monitor and manage these elements allows administrators to optimize system performance, troubleshoot issues, and ensure that resources are being utilized efficiently.

Linux Processes

A process is an instance of a running program. Each process is identified by a unique process ID (PID).

Types of Processes:

- User Processes: Initiated by users, typically associated with applications or scripts.
- System Processes: Started by the operating system during boot, essential for system functionality.
- Daemon Processes: Background processes that typically handle tasks such as web server management, scheduling, and logging.

Viewing and Managing Processes

ps Command:

 - Usage: Displays information about currently running processes.

- Common Options:

- `ps aux`: Lists all processes with detailed information (user, PID, CPU usage, memory usage, etc.).

- `ps -e`: Displays every process on the system.

top Command:

- Usage: Provides a real-time, dynamic view of running processes, including their resource usage.

- Features:

  - Interactive sorting based on CPU, memory usage, etc.

  - Ability to kill processes directly from the interface.

htop Command:

- Usage: An enhanced, interactive version of `top` with a more user-friendly interface.

- Features:

  - Visual representation of CPU and memory usage.

  - Easy navigation and process management.

kill Command:

- Usage: Terminates a process by sending it a signal.

- Common Usage:

  - `kill PID`: Sends a SIGTERM signal to gracefully terminate a process.

  - `kill -9 PID`: Sends a SIGKILL signal to forcibly terminate a process.

System Resources

CPU Usage:

  - Monitoring: Check CPU utilization using `top`, `htop`, or `mpstat`.

  - Optimization: Identify high CPU usage processes and optimize or terminate them if necessary.

Memory Usage:

  - Monitoring: Use `free -h` to display memory usage in a human-readable format.

  - Optimization: Identify memory leaks or high memory usage processes using `top` or `htop`.

Disk Usage:

  - Monitoring: Use `df -h` to view disk usage across mounted filesystems.

  - Optimization: Clean up unnecessary files, logs, and temporary files using `du` and `find` commands.

Monitoring System Performance

System Load:

Represents the average number of processes waiting to be executed. A high load average indicates potential performance issues.

- Monitoring: Use `uptime` or `top` to view the load average. Compare it against the number of CPU cores to assess system health.

- I/O Performance:

  - Monitoring: Use `iostat` to monitor I/O performance, including read/write rates and device utilization.

  - Optimization: Identify bottlenecks in disk I/O and take corrective actions, such as optimizing disk usage or adding more storage.

Network Usage:

  - Monitoring: Use tools like `iftop`, `nload`, or `netstat` to monitor network traffic and identify bandwidth usage.

  - Optimization: Analyze network activity to detect and address issues such as congestion, unauthorized access, or misconfigured services.

Logging and System Monitoring Tools

syslog:

  - Usage: The default logging system for capturing system messages and logs from various services.

Log Files:

  - `/var/log/syslog`: General system log.

  - `/var/log/auth.log`: Authentication-related events.

  - `/var/log/kern.log`: Kernel messages.

dmesg:

 - Usage: Displays messages from the kernel ring buffer, useful for troubleshooting hardware issues.

 - Command: `dmesg | less` to scroll through the output.

System Monitoring Tools:

 - Nagios/Zabbix: Comprehensive monitoring solutions for tracking system performance, uptime, and alerting.

SAR (System Activity Report):

 - Usage: Collects, reports, and saves system activity information.

 - Command: `sar -u 1 3` to report CPU usage every second, three times.

Automating System Monitoring

Scheduling Monitoring Tasks:

 - cron Jobs:

   - Usage: Schedule regular system monitoring tasks using cron.

   - Example: Set up a cron job to run a system health check script daily.

Automated Alerts:

 - Implement tools like `Monit` to automatically send alerts based on specific criteria (e.g., CPU usage exceeds a threshold).

Network Configuration and Management

Setting Up and Managing Network Interfaces

Effective network configuration and management are crucial for ensuring that a Linux system can communicate with other devices and networks. This chapter focuses on setting up and managing network interfaces, which are the gateways through which a system connects to the network.

Introduction to Network Interfaces

A network interface is a software representation of a physical or virtual network device that allows a system to communicate over a network.

Types of Network Interfaces:

- Ethernet (eth0, eth1, etc.): Wired network interfaces.
- Wireless (wlan0, wlan1, etc.): Wireless network interfaces for Wi-Fi connections.
- Loopback (lo): A special interface used for internal communication within the system.
- Virtual Interfaces (tun, tap, etc.): Interfaces used by virtual machines or VPNs.

Viewing and Identifying Network Interfaces

ifconfig Command:

  - Usage: Displays information about all network interfaces.

- Command: `ifconfig -a` to list all interfaces, including those that are inactive.

ip Command:

   - Usage: A more modern and versatile tool for managing network interfaces.

   - Command: `ip a` or `ip addr` to display detailed information about network interfaces.

Configuring Network Interfaces

Static IP Configuration:

   - Purpose: Assigning a fixed IP address to a network interface.

   - Configuration File: `/etc/network/interfaces` or `/etc/netplan/` (for systems using Netplan).

Example Configuration:

```bash
auto eth0
iface eth0 inet static
address 192.168.1.100
netmask 255.255.255.0
gateway 192.168.1.1
```

   - Applying Changes: Use `ifdown eth0` and `ifup eth0` to restart the interface or `netplan apply` for systems using Netplan.

Dynamic IP Configuration (DHCP):

- Purpose: Automatically assigning an IP address to a network interface from a DHCP server.

- Configuration File: Similar to static IP, but the configuration will specify `dhcp` instead of `static`.

- Example Configuration:

```bash
auto eth0

iface eth0 inet dhcp

```

- **DHCP Client Tool**: `dhclient` can be used to manually request a DHCP lease.

Managing Network Interfaces

Bringing Interfaces Up and Down:

- Commands:

  - `ifup eth0`: Activates the network interface.

  - `ifdown eth0`: Deactivates the network interface.

  - `ip link set eth0 up`: Brings the interface up.

  - `ip link set eth0 down`: Brings the interface down.

Viewing Active Network Interfaces:

  - Command: `ip link show` or `ifconfig` to list currently active interfaces.

Renaming Network Interfaces:

  - Command: Use `ip link set eth0 name newname` to rename an interface.

  - Persistent Naming: Modify `/etc/udev/rules.d/70-persistent-net.rules` for permanent changes.

Configuring Advanced Networking Options

Bonding and Teaming:

  - Purpose: Combine multiple network interfaces to act as one for redundancy and increased bandwidth.

  - Configuration: Edit `/etc/network/interfaces` or use tools like `nmcli` for NetworkManager-based systems.

Example Bonding Configuration:

```bash
auto bond0

iface bond0 inet static

address 192.168.1.101

netmask 255.255.255.0

gateway 192.168.1.1

bond-slaves eth0 eth1
```

```
bond-mode 802.3ad

bond-miimon 100

```
```

Bridging:

- Purpose: Create a virtual network bridge to connect multiple network interfaces.

- Use Case: Common in virtualized environments where virtual machines need to connect to the network.

Configuration:

```bash
auto br0

iface br0 inet static

address 192.168.1.102

netmask 255.255.255.0

bridge_ports eth0 eth1

```

Troubleshooting Network Interfaces

Checking Interface Status:

- Command: `ip link show` or `ifconfig` to verify whether an interface is up or down.

Diagnosing Connectivity Issues:
```

- ping: Tests connectivity to another device or network.

- traceroute: Traces the path packets take to reach their destination.

- mtr: Combines the functionality of `ping` and `traceroute` for continuous monitoring.

Resolving Common Issues:

- No IP Address Assigned: Ensure DHCP is correctly configured or that the static IP is correctly set.

- Interface Not Coming Up: Check for configuration errors, hardware issues, or cable connections.

Understanding and Configuring Firewalls (Iptables, Firewalld)

Firewalls are crucial components of network security, acting as gatekeepers that control the traffic entering and leaving a system. In Linux, firewalls can be managed using tools like `iptables` and `firewalld`. This section provides an in-depth understanding of these tools and guides you through configuring them to secure your Linux environment.

Firewalls

A firewall is a security system that monitors and controls incoming and outgoing network traffic based on predetermined security rules.

Firewalls help protect your system from unauthorized access, malicious attacks, and data breaches by filtering traffic and blocking potentially harmful connections.

iptables

`iptables` is a command-line tool used to configure the Linux kernel's built-in firewall. It allows you to set up, maintain, and inspect tables of IP packet filter rules.

-How iptables Works

iptables uses tables to define different sets of rules. The most common table is the `filter` table, used for general-purpose filtering.

Each table contains chains, which are lists of rules that define how packets should be handled. The most common chains are:

- INPUT: Handles incoming packets.
- OUTPUT: Handles outgoing packets.
- FORWARD: Handles packets being routed through the system.

Rules: Each chain contains rules that define the actions to be taken on matching packets. Rules specify conditions such as source IP, destination IP, port number, and protocol.

Basic iptables Configuration

Installing iptables:

 - Command: `sudo apt-get install iptables` for Debian-based systems or `sudo yum install iptables` for Red Hat-based systems.

Viewing Current Rules:

 - Command: `sudo iptables -L` lists all rules in the filter table.

Creating Simple Rules:

 - Allowing Traffic:

```bash
sudo iptables -A INPUT -p tcp --dport 22 -j ACCEPT
```

This command allows incoming SSH traffic on port 22.

 - Blocking Traffic:

```bash

sudo iptables -A INPUT -p tcp --dport 80 -j DROP

```

This command blocks incoming HTTP traffic on port 80.

- Saving and Restoring iptables Rules:

  - Saving Rules:

    ```bash

    sudo iptables-save > /etc/iptables/rules.v4

    ```

  - Restoring Rules:

    ```bash

    sudo iptables-restore < /etc/iptables/rules.v4

    ```

Introduction to firewalld

`firewalld` is a dynamic firewall management tool with support for network/firewall zones that define the trust level of network connections or interfaces.

Key Features:

  - Zones: firewalld uses zones to define levels of trust for network connections. Each zone has its own set of rules.

- Services: firewalld can easily allow or block services by name, such as `http`, `https`, or `ssh`.

- Rich Rules: firewalld supports complex rules, known as rich rules, that offer more granular control over traffic.

Basic firewalld Configuration

Installing firewalld:

- Command: `sudo apt-get install firewalld` for Debian-based systems or `sudo yum install firewalld` for Red Hat-based systems.

Starting and Enabling firewalld:

- Command:

```bash
sudo systemctl start firewalld

sudo systemctl enable firewalld
```

Checking firewalld Status:

- Command: `sudo firewall-cmd --state` to verify if firewalld is running.

Viewing Current Configuration:

- Command: `sudo firewall-cmd --list-all` to display the active zone and its rules.

Configuring firewalld

Assigning Interfaces to Zones:

- Command:

```bash
sudo firewall-cmd --zone=public --add-interface=eth0 --permanent
```

This command assigns the `eth0` interface to the `public` zone.

Allowing or Blocking Services:

- Allowing a Service:

```bash
sudo firewall-cmd --zone=public --add-service=http --permanent
```

- Blocking a Service:

```bash
sudo firewall-cmd --zone=public --remove-service=http --permanent
```

- Reloading firewalld:

```bash

sudo firewall-cmd --reload

```

- Adding Rich Rules:

  - Example:

  ```bash

  sudo firewall-cmd --zone=public --add-rich-rule='rule
family="ipv4" source address="192.168.1.100" service
name="ssh" accept' --permanent

  ```

  This rule allows SSH traffic only from the IP address
`192.168.1.100`.

Advanced Firewall Configuration

Port Forwarding:

  - iptables:

  ```bash

  sudo iptables -t nat -A PREROUTING -p tcp --dport 8080 -j
REDIRECT --to-port 80

  ```

  - firewalld:

  ```bash
  ```

```bash
sudo firewall-cmd --zone=public --add-forward-port=port=8080:proto=tcp:toport=80
```

Logging Dropped Packets:

- iptables:

```bash
sudo iptables -A INPUT -j LOG --log-prefix "iptables-dropped: "
```

- firewalld:

```bash
sudo firewall-cmd --set-log-denied=all
```

Troubleshooting Firewalls

Common Issues:

- Blocked Traffic: Verify rules and ensure that required services are allowed.

- Misconfigured Rules: Check for typos or incorrect parameters in rules.

Commands for Troubleshooting:

- iptables: Use `sudo iptables -L -v -n` for verbose output to understand which rules are being applied.

- firewalld: Use `sudo firewall-cmd --list-all-zones` to review the configuration of all zones.

Troubleshooting Network Issues

Network issues can be some of the most challenging problems to diagnose and resolve on a Linux system. This section provides a systematic approach to troubleshooting network issues, covering common problems, diagnostic tools, and practical solutions.

Common Network Issues

- No Internet Connection: Often caused by incorrect network configuration, DNS issues, or hardware problems.
- Slow Network Performance: Can result from network congestion, faulty cables, or misconfigured settings.
- **Intermittent Connectivity: Frequently due to unstable network drivers, weak Wi-Fi signals, or external interference.
- DNS Resolution Failures: May arise from misconfigured DNS settings or issues with the DNS server itself.
- Firewall Blocking: Incorrect firewall rules can block legitimate traffic, causing network disruptions.

Initial Diagnostics

Check Physical Connections:

- Ensure all cables are securely connected.

- Verify that the network interface card (NIC) is properly seated and functioning.

Restart Networking Services:

- Restart the network service to resolve temporary issues:

```bash
sudo systemctl restart network.service
```

Reboot the System:

- Sometimes a simple reboot can resolve network issues caused by transient errors.

Checking Network Interfaces

List Network Interfaces:

- Use the `ip` or `ifconfig` command to list active network interfaces:

```bash
ip addr show
```

or

```bash
ifconfig
```

```
```

Check Interface Status:

- Ensure the interface is up and running:

```bash
sudo ip link set eth0 up
```

Replace `eth0` with your interface name.

Diagnosing Connectivity Issues

Ping Command:

- Ping the local gateway to check if the system can reach it:

```bash
ping -c 4 192.168.1.1
```

Replace `192.168.1.1` with your gateway IP.

- Ping a public IP (e.g., Google DNS):

```bash
ping -c 4 8.8.8.8
```

If this succeeds, the issue is likely with DNS.

Traceroute Command:

- Trace the path packets take to reach a destination:

```bash

traceroute google.com

```

This helps identify where packets are being dropped or delayed.

Diagnosing DNS Issues

Check DNS Configuration:

- Verify DNS server settings in `/etc/resolv.conf`:

```bash

cat /etc/resolv.conf

```

Ensure the correct nameserver IP addresses are listed.

Test DNS Resolution:

- Use `nslookup` or `dig` to test DNS resolution:

```bash

nslookup google.com

```

or

```bash
```

dig google.com
```
```

Try an Alternative DNS Server:

 - Temporarily switch to a different DNS server, like Google's `8.8.8.8`, to rule out DNS server issues.

Analyzing Network Traffic

tcpdump:

 - Capture and analyze network traffic to diagnose issues:

```bash
sudo tcpdump -i eth0
```

Replace `eth0` with your interface name. Analyze the output for unusual traffic or errors.

Wireshark:

 - A more user-friendly tool for analyzing network traffic. Install and run Wireshark to visually inspect packet flows and identify potential issues.

Firewall and Security Issues

Check iptables Rules:

- Review `iptables` rules to ensure they are not blocking legitimate traffic:

```bash
sudo iptables -L -v -n
```

Review firewalld Configuration:

- Check the active zone and its rules using:

```bash
sudo firewall-cmd --list-all
```

Temporarily Disable the Firewall:

- To determine if the firewall is causing issues, temporarily disable it:

```bash
sudo systemctl stop firewalld
```

or

```bash
sudo iptables -F
```

If connectivity is restored, re-enable the firewall and adjust the rules accordingly.

Advanced Troubleshooting Techniques

Check Routing Tables:

  - Ensure the system's routing table is correct:

   ```bash
   ip route show
   ```

   Look for incorrect or missing routes.

Check Logs:

  - Review system logs for network-related errors:

   ```bash
   sudo journalctl -xe
   ```

   or check specific logs in `/var/log/`.

Reset Network Configuration:

  - If all else fails, reset the network configuration to defaults and reconfigure it from scratch.

Tools for Network Troubleshooting

- nmap:

  - Network scanning tool to discover hosts and services on a network:

  ```bash
  nmap -sP 192.168.1.0/24
  ```

  Replace the IP range with your network's range.

- netstat:

  - Display network connections, routing tables, and interface statistics:

  ```bash
  netstat -tuln
  ```

- ss:

  - Another tool to investigate socket statistics and active connections:

  ```bash
  ss -tuln
  ```

Storage Management

Effective storage management is crucial for maintaining a reliable and efficient Linux system, especially in environments where data integrity and availability are paramount. Let's explore the fundamental concepts and tools necessary for managing storage in Linux, including partitions, file systems, disk quotas, and logical volume management (LVM).

Understanding Linux File Systems

A file system is the method and data structure that an operating system uses to control how data is stored and retrieved. Without a file system, data placed in storage would be one large body of data with no way to tell where one piece of information stops and the next begins.

Common Linux File Systems:

- ext4: The most widely used file system in Linux, known for its stability, performance, and extensive features.
- XFS: A high-performance journaling file system suitable for large files and parallel I/O operations.
- Btrfs: A modern file system that supports advanced features like snapshots, self-healing, and dynamic inode allocation.
- NTFS and exFAT: Used for compatibility with Windows systems, often in dual-boot environments.

Disk Partitioning

Disk partitioning involves dividing a physical disk into separate, logical sections, each of which can be managed independently. This is useful for organizing data, improving performance, and isolating different types of data.

Partitioning Tools:

- fdisk: A command-line tool for creating and managing disk partitions.
- parted: A more advanced tool that supports both MBR and GPT partition tables.
- GParted: A graphical interface for partition management, useful for users who prefer a visual approach.

Creating and Managing Partitions:

Steps to create a new partition using `fdisk`:

```bash
sudo fdisk /dev/sda
```

Replace `/dev/sda` with your disk's identifier.

- After creating partitions, they must be formatted with a file system (e.g., ext4, XFS).

Mounting and Unmounting File Systems

The process of attaching a file system to the Linux directory tree. Once mounted, the file system becomes accessible as part of the overall file structure.

Command to mount a file system:

```bash
sudo mount /dev/sda1 /mnt
```

Replace `/dev/sda1` with your partition and `/mnt` with the desired mount point.

Unmounting File Systems:

To safely remove a file system from the directory tree, unmount it:

```bash
sudo umount /mnt
```

Automating Mounts with fstab:

The `/etc/fstab` file is used to define which file systems should be automatically mounted at boot time. Entries include the device name, mount point, file system type, and mount options.

Logical Volume Management (LVM)

LVM allows for flexible disk management by abstracting the physical storage into logical volumes. It simplifies tasks such as resizing partitions, creating snapshots, and managing multiple disks.

LVM Components:

- Physical Volumes (PV): The raw disk or partition that is initialized for use with LVM.
- Volume Groups (VG): A pool of physical volumes that can be managed as a single entity.
- Logical Volumes (LV): The virtual partitions that are created within a volume group and can be resized or moved easily.

Creating and Managing LVM:

- Initializing Physical Volumes:

```bash
sudo pvcreate /dev/sdb1
```

Creating a Volume Group:

```bash
sudo vgcreate my_vg /dev/sdb1
```

Replace `my_vg` with the desired volume group name.

Creating a Logical Volume:

```bash
sudo lvcreate -L 10G -n my_lv my_vg
```

Replace `10G` with the desired size and `my_lv` with the logical volume name.

- Resizing Logical Volumes:
  - Expanding:

    ```bash
    sudo lvextend -L +5G /dev/my_vg/my_lv
    sudo resize2fs /dev/my_vg/my_lv
    ```

  - Reducing:

    ```bash
    sudo lvreduce -L -5G /dev/my_vg/my_lv
    sudo resize2fs /dev/my_vg/my_lv
    ```

Managing Disk Quotas

Disk quotas are used to limit the amount of disk space or number of files a user or group can use, which is essential for managing resources on shared systems.

Setting Up Quotas:

Enable quotas on a file system by adding `usrquota` and/or `grpquota` options in `/etc/fstab`.

- Initialize the quota database:

```bash
sudo quotacheck -cug /mountpoint
```

- Assign quotas using `edquota`:

```bash
sudo edquota username
```

Monitoring and Managing Quotas:

- View quota usage with `quota`:

```bash
quota -u username
```

Disk Monitoring and Maintenance

Checking Disk Usage:

 - The `df` command provides an overview of disk usage across all mounted file systems:

```bash
df -h
```

Analyzing Disk Space:

 - The `du` command helps to identify which directories are consuming the most space:

```bash
du -sh /path/to/directory
```

Monitoring Disk Health:

 - Tools like `smartctl` can be used to monitor the health of hard drives and predict potential failures:

```bash
sudo smartctl -a /dev/sda
```

Partitioning and Formatting Disks

Efficient disk management is fundamental for maintaining the performance, reliability, and organization of a Linux system. Partitioning and formatting disks are fundamental tasks in managing a Linux system. This process involves dividing a disk into distinct sections (partitions) and preparing these partitions with file systems so that data can be stored and retrieved efficiently. Here's a detailed guide on how to partition and format disks in Linux.

Disk partitioning is the process of dividing a physical disk into multiple logical sections, known as partitions. Each partition can be treated as a separate disk, with its own file system and purpose. Partitioning allows you to organize data, optimize performance, and maintain different operating systems or data types on the same disk.

Types of Partitions:

- Primary Partition: A disk can have up to four primary partitions. These are the main partitions that can hold data or an operating system.
- Extended Partition: If more than four partitions are needed, one of the primary partitions can be converted into an extended partition, which can then contain multiple logical partitions.
- Logical Partition: Partitions within an extended partition are called logical partitions. These allow for more flexibility in organizing disk space.

Partition Table Types:

- MBR (Master Boot Record): The older type of partition table, supporting up to four primary partitions and disk sizes up to 2TB.

- GPT (GUID Partition Table): A modern partition table that supports a larger number of partitions (up to 128) and disk sizes larger than 2TB.

Tools for Partitioning Disks

fdisk:

A command-line utility for partitioning disks that works well with MBR partitions.

- Example of launching `fdisk`:

```bash
sudo fdisk /dev/sda
```

Replace `/dev/sda` with the identifier of your disk.

parted:

A more advanced command-line tool that supports both MBR and GPT partitions.

- Example of launching `parted`:

```bash
```

sudo parted /dev/sda

```
```

GParted:

A graphical tool that provides a visual interface for partitioning disks. It is user-friendly and ideal for those who prefer a GUI over command-line tools.

Creating and Managing Partitions

Step-by-Step Partitioning Using `fdisk`:

Launch `fdisk`:

```bash
sudo fdisk /dev/sda
```

Create a New Partition:

- Enter `n` to create a new partition.

- Choose between primary (`p`) or extended (`e`) partition.

- Specify the partition number and sectors (you can use defaults).

Write the Changes:

- After creating partitions, enter `w` to write the changes to the disk.

Creating GPT Partitions with `parted`:

Launch `parted`:

```bash
sudo parted /dev/sda
```

Set the Partition Table to GPT:

```bash
mklabel gpt
```

Create a New Partition:

```bash
mkpart primary ext4 1MiB 100%
```

This creates a primary partition using the `ext4` file system, from 1MB to the end of the disk.

Quit `parted`:

```bash
quit
```

Formatting Partitions with File Systems

Formatting a partition involves setting up a file system on it, which organizes how data is stored and retrieved. Without formatting, a partition cannot be used to store data.

Common File Systems:

- ext4: The most commonly used file system in Linux, known for its reliability and performance.
- XFS: Suitable for handling large files and parallel I/O operations.
- Btrfs: A modern file system that includes features like snapshots and self-healing.
- NTFS: Used mainly for compatibility with Windows systems.

Formatting a Partition

Using `mkfs` to Format:

- For `ext4`:

```bash
sudo mkfs.ext4 /dev/sda1
```

Replace `/dev/sda1` with your partition identifier.

- For `XFS`:

```bash
sudo mkfs.xfs /dev/sda1
```

Verifying the File System:

- Use the `blkid` command to verify the file system:

```bash
sudo blkid /dev/sda1
```

Mounting and Using the Partition

Mounting the Partition:

- To use the formatted partition, it needs to be mounted to the Linux directory structure.

- Example:

```bash
sudo mount /dev/sda1 /mnt
```

Replace `/mnt` with the desired mount point.

- **Persistent Mounting with `/etc/fstab`:**

- To ensure the partition mounts automatically at boot, add an entry to `/etc/fstab`:

```bash
```

/dev/sda1 /mnt ext4 defaults 0 2

```
```

Managing and Resizing Partitions

Resizing a Partition:

 - If you need to resize a partition, you can use tools like `parted` or `resize2fs` (for ext4).

 - Example using `resize2fs`:

```bash
```

sudo resize2fs /dev/sda1 20G

```
```

This resizes the file system to 20GB. Ensure the partition is unmounted before resizing.

Deleting a Partition:

 - To delete a partition using `fdisk`:

```bash
```

sudo fdisk /dev/sda

```
```

Enter `d` and select the partition number to delete.

Managing Volumes and File Systems

In Linux, managing volumes and file systems is a fundamental aspect of system administration. Proper management ensures efficient storage utilization, data integrity, and overall system performance. This section will cover key concepts and techniques for handling volumes and file systems, including creating, mounting, and maintaining them.

Understanding Volumes and File Systems

Volumes:

A volume is a single accessible storage area with a file system. It can be as simple as a single disk partition or as complex as a Logical Volume (LV) spread across multiple disks.

File Systems:

A file system is a way of organizing and storing files on a storage device. Common file systems in Linux include ext4, XFS, Btrfs, and others, each with its strengths and use cases.

Creating and Managing Volumes

Logical Volume Management (LVM):

LVM provides flexibility by allowing you to manage disk space more efficiently. It abstracts physical storage devices into logical volumes, which can be resized, moved, or mirrored without affecting the data stored.

Creating Logical Volumes:

- Start by creating a Physical Volume (PV):

```bash
sudo pvcreate /dev/sdb1
```

- Create a Volume Group (VG):

```bash
sudo vgcreate my_vg /dev/sdb1
```

Create a Logical Volume (LV):

```bash
sudo lvcreate -L 20G -n my_lv my_vg
```


Managing Logical Volumes:

- Extending a Logical Volume:

```bash
sudo lvextend -L +10G /dev/my_vg/my_lv
sudo resize2fs /dev/my_vg/my_lv
```

Reducing a Logical Volume:

```bash
sudo lvreduce -L -5G /dev/my_vg/my_lv

sudo resize2fs /dev/my_vg/my_lv
```

Removing a Logical Volume:

```bash
sudo lvremove /dev/my_vg/my_lv
```

Mounting and Unmounting File Systems

Mounting File Systems:

- After creating a volume, it needs to be mounted to make it accessible. Mounting a file system involves attaching it to a directory in the Linux file system tree.

```bash
sudo mount /dev/sdb1 /mnt
```

- The mount point (`/mnt` in this example) becomes the root of the newly mounted file system.

Unmounting File Systems:

- When a file system is no longer needed, it should be unmounted to safely detach it from the directory tree:

```bash
sudo umount /mnt
```

Persistent Mounts with /etc/fstab:

- To automatically mount a file system at boot, add an entry to `/etc/fstab`:

```
/dev/sdb1 /mnt ext4 defaults 0 2
```

Maintaining File Systems

Checking and Repairing File Systems:

- Regularly check file systems for errors using `fsck` (file system check):

```bash
sudo fsck /dev/sdb1
```

- This command checks and repairs inconsistencies in the file system.

Monitoring Disk Usage:

- Use the `df` command to monitor disk usage:

```bash
df -h
```

- Use `du` to check disk usage for specific directories:

```bash
du -sh /path/to/directory
```

Optimizing File Systems:

- File systems can become fragmented over time. While ext4 and other modern file systems are designed to minimize fragmentation, tools like `e4defrag` can be used to defragment if necessary:

```bash
sudo e4defrag /dev/sdb1
```

Managing File System Types

Choosing the Right File System:

- Different file systems offer various features:

  - ext4: General-purpose file system with good performance and stability.

  - XFS: High-performance file system suitable for large files and parallel I/O.

  - Btrfs: Advanced file system with features like snapshots and subvolumes.

  - ZFS: Known for its data integrity features, often used in high-availability environments.

Formatting a Volume with a File System:

  - To format a volume with a file system, use `mkfs`:

  ```bash
  sudo mkfs.ext4 /dev/sdb1
  ```

  - Replace `ext4` with your desired file system type.

Advanced File System Features

Snapshots (Btrfs, LVM):

  - Snapshots capture the state of a file system at a particular point in time. They are useful for backups and recovering from errors.

Data Compression (Btrfs, ZFS):

- Some file systems, like Btrfs and ZFS, offer built-in data compression to save space.

Understanding Raid and Lvm (Logical Volume Management)

RAID (Redundant Array of Independent Disks) and LVM (Logical Volume Management) are two critical technologies in Linux that provide flexibility, reliability, and performance improvements for managing storage systems. While they serve different purposes, both are often used together in enterprise environments to optimize storage solutions.

RAID (Redundant Array of Independent Disks)

What is RAID?

RAID is a technology that combines multiple physical disk drives into a single logical unit to improve data redundancy, performance, or both. There are several RAID levels, each offering different trade-offs between redundancy (fault tolerance), performance, and storage capacity.

Common RAID Levels:

RAID 0 (Striping):

  - Purpose: Increases performance by splitting data across multiple disks.

  - Pros: High read/write speeds.

  - Cons: No redundancy; if one disk fails, all data is lost.

RAID 1 (Mirroring):

 - Purpose: Provides redundancy by duplicating data across two disks.

 - Pros: High fault tolerance; if one disk fails, data is still accessible.

 - Cons: Storage capacity is halved.

RAID 5 (Striping with Parity):

 - Purpose: Balances performance and redundancy by distributing parity information across disks.

 - Pros: Fault tolerance with efficient storage use; can survive one disk failure.

 - Cons: Slower write performance compared to RAID 0; requires at least three disks.

RAID 6 (Striping with Double Parity):

 - Purpose: Similar to RAID 5, but with additional redundancy.

 - Pros: Can survive two simultaneous disk failures.

 - Cons: Requires at least four disks; slower write performance.

RAID 10 (Combination of RAID 1 and RAID 0):

 - Purpose: Combines the benefits of RAID 0 (performance) and RAID 1 (redundancy).

- Pros: High performance and fault tolerance.

- Cons: Expensive, as it requires at least four disks.

Software vs. Hardware RAID:

Software RAID:

- Managed by the operating system, using tools like `mdadm` in Linux.

- Pros: Cost-effective, flexible.

- Cons: Slightly lower performance compared to hardware RAID.

Hardware RAID:

- Managed by a dedicated RAID controller.

- Pros: Better performance, offloads RAID processing from the CPU.

- Cons: More expensive, potential for controller failure.

Creating a RAID Array in Linux:

- Install `mdadm`:

  ```bash
  sudo apt-get install mdadm
  ```

- Create a RAID 1 array:

```bash

sudo mdadm --create --verbose /dev/md0 --level=1 --raid-
devices=2 /dev/sda /dev/sdb

```

- Monitor and manage RAID arrays with `mdadm`.

LVM (Logical Volume Management)

What is LVM?

LVM is a powerful tool in Linux that allows for flexible disk
management by abstracting physical storage into logical volumes.
It enables easy resizing, moving, and managing disk space,
making it an essential tool for dynamic storage environments.

LVM Components:

Physical Volumes (PV):

 - The physical disks or partitions used in LVM. These are the
building blocks of a volume group.

 - Example:

```bash

sudo pvcreate /dev/sda1
```

```
```

Volume Groups (VG):

- A collection of physical volumes that create a storage pool from which logical volumes are allocated.

- Example:

```bash
sudo vgcreate my_vg /dev/sda1 /dev/sdb1
```

Logical Volumes (LV):

- The virtual partitions created from a volume group. These can be resized or moved without affecting the data.

- Example:

```bash
sudo lvcreate -L 50G -n my_lv my_vg
```

Benefits of LVM:

Flexibility:

- Easily resize logical volumes without downtime.

- Combine multiple disks into a single logical volume.

Snapshots:

  - Create snapshots of a logical volume for backup purposes.

  - Example:

  ```bash
  sudo lvcreate --size 10G --snapshot --name my_snapshot /dev/my_vg/my_lv
  ```

Ease of Management:

  - Logical volumes can be easily moved to different physical disks.

  - Example:

  ```bash
  sudo pvmove /dev/sda1 /dev/sdb1
  ```

Combining RAID and LVM:

RAID and LVM can be used together to combine the benefits of both technologies. For example, RAID can be used to provide redundancy and performance, while LVM adds flexibility in managing storage.

Example Setup:

- Create a RAID 5 array across three disks.

- Use the RAID array as a physical volume in LVM.

- Create volume groups and logical volumes on top of the RAID array for added flexibility.

Security and Hardening

Security is a crucial aspect of managing Linux systems, especially in environments where data integrity, confidentiality, and availability are paramount. This chapter covers various techniques and best practices to secure and harden your Linux system against potential threats. The goal is to minimize vulnerabilities and ensure that your system remains resilient against attacks.

Importance of Security in Linux

Linux is widely recognized for its security features, but no system is invulnerable. Securing a Linux environment involves multiple layers, from network defenses to system configurations. By applying security best practices and hardening techniques, administrators can significantly reduce the risk of breaches and ensure that their systems are protected from both external and internal threats.

Basic Security Practices

Regular Updates and Patch Management

Keeping your system up-to-date is one of the most effective ways to protect against known vulnerabilities. Outdated software can be exploited by attackers.

How to Implement:

  - Use your package manager (e.g., APT, YUM, DNF) to regularly update all packages.

- Enable automatic updates for critical security patches.

- Example command for APT-based systems:

```bash
sudo apt-get update && sudo apt-get upgrade
```

Secure User Account Management

Principle of Least Privilege: Users should only have the permissions necessary to perform their tasks. Avoid using the root account for routine activities.

How to Implement:

- Use the `sudo` command to grant temporary administrative privileges.

- Create separate accounts for different users and assign appropriate roles.

- Example of adding a user with limited privileges:

```bash
sudo adduser newuser
sudo usermod -aG sudo newuser
```

Password Policies

Weak passwords are a common attack vector. Enforcing strong password policies reduces the risk of unauthorized access.

How to Implement:

- Require complex passwords (a mix of letters, numbers, and special characters).

- Use `passwd` to enforce password expiration and complexity:

```bash
sudo passwd -x 90 -n 7 -w 7 newuser
```

- Implement two-factor authentication (2FA) for added security.

Hardening the Linux System

Configuring the Firewall

A firewall controls incoming and outgoing network traffic, providing a critical layer of defense against unauthorized access.

- Tools: Use `iptables` or `firewalld` to configure firewall rules.
  - iptables:

```bash
sudo iptables -A INPUT -p tcp --dport 22 -j ACCEPT
sudo iptables -A INPUT -j DROP
```

  - firewalld:

```bash
sudo firewall-cmd --add-port=22/tcp --permanent

sudo firewall-cmd --reload
```

Best Practices: Close all unnecessary ports, allow only trusted IP addresses, and log dropped packets for monitoring.

Securing SSH

SSH is a common target for brute-force attacks. Hardening SSH access can prevent unauthorized remote logins.

How to Implement:

- Change the default SSH port:

```bash
sudo nano /etc/ssh/sshd_config

# Change the line:

Port 22
```

- Disable root login:

```bash
sudo nano /etc/ssh/sshd_config
```

```
# Change the line:

PermitRootLogin no

```
```

- Use SSH keys instead of passwords:

  ```bash
  ssh-keygen -t rsa -b 4096

  ssh-copy-id user@server
  ```

  - Enable two-factor authentication (2FA)** for SSH.

File and Directory Permissions

Proper file and directory permissions prevent unauthorized users from accessing or modifying sensitive files.

How to Implement:

 - Use `chmod` to set file permissions.

 - Use `chown` to change file ownership.

 - Example:

   ```bash
   sudo chmod 700 /sensitive_directory

   sudo chown root:root /sensitive_directory
   ```
   ```

```
```

Best Practices: Set restrictive permissions by default and only grant broader permissions when necessary.

Auditing and Monitoring

Continuous monitoring and auditing of system activities help detect and respond to potential security incidents.

- Tools:

  - Auditd: A Linux auditing tool that records security-relevant events.

  ```bash
  sudo apt-get install auditd
  sudo auditctl -a always,exit -F arch=b64 -S execve
  ```

  - Logwatch: Analyzes system logs and generates daily reports.

  ```bash
  sudo apt-get install logwatch
  sudo logwatch --detail High --mailto admin@example.com --range today
  ```

Best Practices: Regularly review logs, set up alerts for suspicious activity, and conduct periodic security audits.

Advanced Security Measures

SELinux and AppArmor

SELinux: Security-Enhanced Linux (SELinux) enforces mandatory access controls (MAC) to limit what processes can do on the system.

- Commands:

```bash
sudo setenforce 1   # Enable SELinux

sudo getenforce     # Check SELinux status
```

AppArmor: Similar to SELinux, AppArmor uses profiles to restrict the capabilities of individual programs.

- Commands:

```bash
sudo aa-status      # Check AppArmor status

sudo aa-enforce /etc/apparmor.d/usr.sbin.mysqld  # Enforce a profile
```

Intrusion Detection Systems (IDS)

IDS helps detect unauthorized access or changes to the system.

- Tools:

  - OSSEC: A host-based IDS for monitoring and alerting.

    ```bash
    sudo apt-get install ossec-hids
    ```

  - Tripwire: Monitors files and directories for unauthorized changes.

    ```bash
    sudo apt-get install tripwire
    ```

Best Practices: Regularly update IDS rules, monitor alerts, and respond to potential incidents promptly.

Physical Security Considerations

Physical security is as important as digital security. Unauthorized physical access can lead to data breaches or system tampering.

Best Practices:

- Secure Server Rooms: Restrict access to server rooms with biometric locks or key cards.
- Use BIOS/UEFI Passwords: Prevent unauthorized access to system BIOS/UEFI settings.

- Encrypt Disk Drives: Use tools like LUKS to encrypt disk drives, protecting data at rest.

Securing and hardening a Linux system requires a comprehensive approach, addressing both common vulnerabilities and advanced threats. By implementing the techniques outlined in this chapter, administrators can significantly enhance the security posture of their Linux environments, ensuring that their systems remain resilient in the face of evolving security challenges.

Regular Security Audits and Patching

Regular security audits and timely patching are fundamental practices in maintaining a secure and resilient Linux system. These processes help identify and remediate vulnerabilities, ensure compliance with security standards, and protect against emerging threats. This section delves into the importance of security audits and patch management, outlining best practices, tools, and methodologies to effectively secure your Linux environment.

What are Security Audits?

A security audit is a systematic evaluation of a system's security posture. It involves assessing the system against predefined standards and policies to identify vulnerabilities, misconfigurations, and compliance issues. Security audits help organizations understand their security weaknesses and implement appropriate measures to mitigate risks.

What is Patching?

Patching involves updating software and systems to fix security vulnerabilities, bugs, and improve functionality. Patches are released by software vendors to address known issues that could be exploited by attackers. Regular patching ensures that systems are protected against the latest threats and operate efficiently.

Importance of Regular Audits and Patching

- Risk Mitigation: Identifies and addresses vulnerabilities before they can be exploited.
- Compliance: Ensures adherence to security standards and regulations (e.g., PCI DSS, HIPAA).
- System Stability: Maintains optimal performance and reliability of systems.
- Trust and Reputation: Protects organizational data and maintains stakeholder confidence.

CONDUCTING REGULAR SECURITY AUDITS

Regular security audits involve a comprehensive assessment of your Linux systems using various tools and methodologies. The process can be broken down into several key steps:

Planning and Preparation

- Define Scope: Determine which systems, applications, and networks will be audited.

- Establish Objectives: Set clear goals for what the audit aims to achieve.
- Gather Documentation: Collect system configurations, policies, and previous audit reports.
- Assign Roles and Responsibilities: Identify team members and their specific tasks.

Types of Security Audits

- Internal Audits: Conducted by internal staff to assess and improve security measures.
- External Audits: Performed by third-party auditors to provide an unbiased evaluation.
- Compliance Audits: Focus on meeting specific regulatory requirements.
- Vulnerability Assessments: Identify and prioritize security weaknesses.

Security Audit Process

Information Gathering

- **Asset Inventory**: Document all hardware and software assets.
- **Network Mapping**: Identify network topology and connected devices.
- **User Accounts and Permissions**: Review user access levels and privileges.

Vulnerability Scanning

Use automated tools to scan systems for known vulnerabilities.

Common Tools:

Nessus: A comprehensive vulnerability scanner.

```bash
# Running a Nessus scan (requires Nessus installation)
nessus -q -x -T html -o scan_report.html target_ip
```

OpenVAS: An open-source vulnerability assessment tool.

```bash
# Starting an OpenVAS scan
openvas-start
```

- **Nmap**: Network exploration and security auditing tool.

```bash
nmap -sV -O target_ip
```

Configuration Review

System Configurations: Check for secure settings in system files (e.g., `/etc/ssh/sshd_config`).

Service Hardening: Ensure services are configured with security best practices.

Firewall Rules: Verify that firewall configurations adhere to security policies.

Access Control Assessment

User Accounts: Identify and remove unnecessary or inactive accounts.

Permission Checks: Ensure files and directories have appropriate permissions.

```bash
# Finding world-writable files
find / -type f -perm -o+w -exec ls -l {} \;
```

Sudoers Review: Audit the `/etc/sudoers` file for proper privilege delegation.

Log Analysis

- System Logs: Review logs for suspicious activities or anomalies.

```bash
```

```bash
sudo tail -f /var/log/auth.log
```

Automated Tools:

- Logwatch: Summarizes and reports on system logs.

```bash
sudo logwatch --detail High --mailto admin@example.com --range today
```

- OSSEC: Monitors logs and file integrity.

```bash
sudo ossec-control start
```

Penetration Testing

Simulate attacks to evaluate the effectiveness of security measures.

Tools:

- Metasploit Framework: For developing and executing exploit code.

```bash
msfconsole
```

```
```

- Hydra: For brute-force password testing.

```bash
hydra -l user -P /path/to/wordlist.txt target_ip ssh
```

Documentation and Reporting

Findings Report: Document all discovered vulnerabilities and issues.

Risk Assessment: Evaluate the severity and potential impact of each finding.

Recommendations: Provide actionable steps to remediate identified issues.

Remediation and Follow-up

- Implement Fixes: Address vulnerabilities based on priority.

- Verification: Re-scan and test systems to ensure issues have been resolved.

- Continuous Monitoring: Set up systems for ongoing security monitoring.

Security Audit Tools

Lynis

An open-source security auditing tool for Unix-based systems.

Features:

- System and network scanning.

- Compliance testing.

- Suggestions for hardening.

Usage:

```bash
sudo apt-get install lynis

sudo lynis audit system
```


OpenSCAP

A collection of tools for compliance auditing.

Features:

- Security Content Automation Protocol (SCAP) scanning.

- Compliance checks against standards like PCI-DSS, HIPAA.

Usage:

```bash
sudo apt-get install openscap-utils scap-security-guide

sudo oscap xccdf eval --profile
xccdf_org.ssgproject.content_profile_pci-dss
/usr/share/xml/scap/ssg/content/ssg-ubuntu1804-ds.xml
```

Auditd

A userspace component to the Linux Auditing System.

Features:

- Tracks system calls and logs events.

- Monitors file access and system changes.

Usage:

```bash
sudo apt-get install auditd

sudo auditctl -w /etc/passwd -p wa -k passwd_changes
```

EFFECTIVE PATCH MANAGEMENT

Patch management is the process of acquiring, testing, and installing patches (code changes) to software and systems. Effective patch management ensures that systems are up-to-date and protected against known vulnerabilities.

Patch Management Process

Inventory Management

  - Identify Assets: Maintain an up-to-date list of all software and hardware.

  - Version Tracking: Keep track of software versions and patch levels.

Patch Identification

  - Monitoring Sources: Regularly check for new patches from vendors and security advisories.

  - Automation Tools: Use tools that automatically notify about available updates.

Patch Evaluation

  - Assess Relevance: Determine if a patch is applicable to your environment.

  - Risk Assessment: Evaluate the severity and potential impact of not applying the patch.

Testing

- Test Environment: Apply patches in a controlled setting to identify potential issues.

- Compatibility Checks: Ensure patches do not disrupt existing services or applications.

Deployment

- Scheduling: Plan patch deployments during maintenance windows to minimize disruption.

- Phased Rollout: Deploy patches gradually across systems to monitor for adverse effects.

- Automation: Use configuration management tools for efficient deployment.

- Ansible Example:

```yaml
---
- hosts: all
  become: yes
  tasks:
    - name: Update all packages to latest
      apt:
        update_cache: yes
        upgrade: dist
```

```
```

Verification

- Post-Deployment Testing: Confirm that patches are applied correctly and systems are functioning as expected.

- Compliance Reporting: Document patch status for auditing and compliance purposes.

Continuous Monitoring

- Vulnerability Scanning: Regularly scan systems to ensure no new vulnerabilities have emerged.

- Feedback Loop: Incorporate lessons learned into future patch management cycles.

Patch Management Tools

Package Managers

- APT (Debian/Ubuntu):

```bash
sudo apt-get update

sudo apt-get upgrade
```

- YUM/DNF (Red Hat/CentOS/Fedora):

  ```bash
  sudo yum check-update
  sudo yum update
  ```

- Zypper (SUSE):

  ```bash
  sudo zypper refresh
  sudo zypper update
  ```

Unattended Upgrades

Automate the installation of security updates.

- Configuration (APT-based systems):

  ```bash
  sudo apt-get install unattended-upgrades
  sudo dpkg-reconfigure unattended-upgrades
  ```

- Customize Settings: Edit `/etc/apt/apt.conf.d/50unattended-upgrades` to specify which updates to apply automatically.

Configuration Management Tools

Ansible, Puppet, Chef, and SaltStack can automate patch deployment across multiple systems.

- Ansible Example Playbook:

```yaml
---
- name: Apply security patches
  hosts: servers
  become: yes
  tasks:
    - name: Update package list
      apt:
        update_cache: yes

    - name: Apply security updates
      apt:
        upgrade: dist
        autoclean: yes
        autoremove: yes
```

WSUS for Linux

Spacewalk and Red Hat Satellite provide centralized patch management similar to Windows Server Update Services (WSUS) but for Linux systems.

Best Practices for Patch Management

- Establish a Patch Policy: Define procedures and responsibilities for patch management.
- Prioritize Patches: Apply critical security patches promptly, while less critical updates can follow scheduled maintenance.
- Maintain Backups: Always backup systems before applying patches to enable recovery in case of issues.
- Document Changes: Keep detailed records of all patches applied, including dates and any issues encountered.
- Stay Informed: Subscribe to security bulletins and alerts from relevant vendors and security organizations.
- Train Staff: Ensure that IT personnel are trained in patch management processes and tools.

Integrating Audits and Patching into Security Strategy

- Continuous Improvement: Use findings from audits to improve patch management processes and overall security posture.
- Policy Enforcement: Ensure that security policies are consistently applied and enforced through regular audits and compliance checks.

- Incident Response Preparedness: Regular audits and patching help in early detection and quick response to security incidents.
- Stakeholder Communication: Keep stakeholders informed about security measures, audit results, and patch management activities.

Regular security audits and effective patch management are essential components of a robust security strategy. By systematically identifying and addressing vulnerabilities through audits and ensuring that systems are consistently updated with the latest patches, organizations can significantly reduce the risk of security breaches and maintain the integrity and reliability of their Linux environments. Implementing these practices requires careful planning, the use of appropriate tools, and a commitment to ongoing vigilance and improvement.

Conclusion

Mastering Linux from installation to advanced system administration equips you with the skills to navigate and manage one of the most powerful and versatile operating systems available. This journey has taken you through the fundamentals of Linux, from understanding its history and significance to mastering complex tasks like network configuration, security hardening, and storage management.

By embracing Linux, you've unlocked the potential to customize and control your computing environment with precision. Whether you're deploying Linux in enterprise settings, managing servers, or simply using it for personal projects, the knowledge gained from this book will serve as a solid foundation for further exploration and expertise.

Linux is continuously evolving, and so should your learning. Stay curious, keep experimenting, and continue to explore the vast world of Linux. The skills you've acquired here will not only enhance your technical abilities but also empower you to contribute to the open-source community and beyond.

Your journey with Linux is just beginning. Keep pushing the boundaries of what's possible, and you'll find that the opportunities with Linux are limitless.

References

Books

- **Hill, B. M., Mako, Y. B., & Baxter, M. (2020).** *The Debian System: Concepts and Techniques.* No Starch Press. ISBN: 978-1593271024.
  Focuses on Debian-based Linux distributions, including Ubuntu, with detailed concepts on package management and system administration.
- **Negus, C. (2020).** *Linux Bible (10th Edition).* Wiley. ISBN: 978-1119578889.
  Offers a thorough introduction to Linux with practical examples, including Ubuntu, Red Hat, and others.

Websites

- **Ubuntu Official Documentation**
  https://help.ubuntu.com/
  The official site for Ubuntu documentation. It covers installation guides, desktop, and server administration, security, and advanced configuration.
- **Linux Documentation Project**
  https://www.tldp.org/
  A vast collection of how-tos, guides, and manuals related to Linux, providing resources for both beginners and advanced users.
- **Ubuntu Community Help Wiki**
  https://help.ubuntu.com/community
  A user-contributed documentation site that offers practical help on various Ubuntu topics.

- **Linux Kernel Archives**
  https://www.kernel.org/
  The official site for Linux kernel releases and updates. A valuable resource for system administrators looking to compile and configure custom kernels.
- **Stack Overflow - Linux/Ubuntu Tags**
  https://stackoverflow.com/questions/tagged/linux
  A popular forum for asking questions and finding solutions to Linux and Ubuntu-specific problems.
- **Ubuntu Forums**
  https://ubuntuforums.org/
  A large and active community forum where Ubuntu users ask questions and share knowledge on everything from installation to advanced system configurations.
- **DigitalOcean Tutorials - Ubuntu**
  https://www.digitalocean.com/community/tutorials/tag/ubuntu
  A vast resource of tutorials related to Ubuntu, covering a wide range of topics like server setup, security, and software installation.

Online Courses

- **Linux Foundation: Introduction to Linux**
  https://training.linuxfoundation.org/training/introduction-to-linux/
  A free online course provided by the Linux Foundation that covers the fundamentals of Linux.
- **edX: Linux System Administration Essentials**
  https://www.edx.org/course/linux-system-administration-essentials
  This course offers essential training for Linux system

administrators, with modules on advanced system configuration and troubleshooting.

Software Tools and Resources

- **GitHub - Ubuntu**
  https://github.com/ubuntu
  The official GitHub repository for Ubuntu development projects.
- **Canonical Livepatch Service**
  https://ubuntu.com/security/livepatch
  A service provided by Canonical that applies security patches to your running Ubuntu system without the need for a reboot. Ideal for servers and critical infrastructure.
- **Advanced Packaging Tool (APT) Documentation**
  https://wiki.debian.org/Apt
  Learn more about APT, the package manager used by Ubuntu, and its functionality in package installation and management.

www.ingramcontent.com/pod-product-compliance
Lightning Source LLC
LaVergne TN
LVHW051231050326
832903LV00028B/2355